DEPRESSION

Recent Titles in
Bibliographies and Indexes in Medical Studies

Federal Information Sources in Health and Medicine:
A Selected Annotated Bibliography
Mary Glen Chitty, compiler, with the assistance of Natalie Schatz

Viruses and Reproduction: A Bibliography
Ernest L. Abel, compiler

The History of Cancer: An Annotated Bibliography
James S. Olson, compiler

New Literature On Fetal Alcohol Exposure and Effects:
A Bibliography, 1983–1988
Ernest L. Abel, compiler

Sociodemographic Factors in the Epidemiology of Multiple
Sclerosis: An Annotated Bibliography
George W. Lowis, compiler

Prostitutes in Medical Literature: An Annotated Bibliography
Sachi Sri Kantha, compiler

Vital and Health Statistics Series: An Annotated Checklist and
Index to the Publications of the "Rainbow Series"
Jim Walsh and A. James Bothmer, compilers

Medicine in Great Britain from the Restoration to the Nineteenth
Century, 1660–1800: An Annotated Bibliography
Samuel J. Rogal, compiler

Treatment of Cocaine Abuse: An Annotated Bibliography
John J. Miletich, compiler

AIDS: A Multimedia Sourcebook
John J. Miletich, compiler

DEPRESSION

A Multimedia Sourcebook

Compiled by John J. Miletich

Foreword by Dan G. Blazer

Bibliographies and Indexes in Medical Studies,
Number 11

GREENWOOD PRESS
Westport, Connecticut • London

Library of Congress Cataloging-in-Publication Data

Miletich, John J.
Depression : a multimedia sourcebook / compiled by John J. Miletich ; foreword by Dan G. Blazer.
p. cm.—(Bibliographies and indexes in medical studies, ISSN 0896–6591 ; no. 11)
Includes bibliographical references and indexes.
ISBN 0–313–29374–0 (alk. paper)
1. Depression, Mental—Bibliography. I. Title. II. Series.
[DNLM: 1. Depressive Disorder—bibliography. ZWM 171 M643d 1995]
Z6665.7.D46M55 1995
[RC537]
016.61685′27—dc20
DNLM/DLC
for Library of Congress 95–4194

British Library Cataloguing in Publication Data is available.

Library of Congress Catalog Card Number: 95–4194
ISBN: 0–313–29374–0
ISSN: 0896–6591

First published in 1995

Greenwood Press, 88 Post Road West, Westport, CT 06881
An imprint of Greenwood Publishing Group, Inc.

Printed in the United States of America

The paper used in this book complies with the Permanent Paper Standard issued by the National Information Standards Organization (Z39.48–1984).

10 9 8 7 6 5 4 3 2 1

To Rob Bateman

CONTENTS

FOREWORD

Depressive disorders are among the most frequent and most disabling of the chronic illnesses which afflict persons of all ages in modern Western society. Much focus has been placed upon the study of depression, ranging from neurobiological to cross-cultural and existential studies. If one were to review even recent publications in a comprehensive index, such as **Index Medicus**, one would be overwhelmed with the number of articles and the lack of clear organization of these articles.

For this reason, I believe John Miletich has provided an important service with the publication of **Depression: A Multimedia Sourcebook.** Though the list is not comprehensive, in my review of the articles, I believe John Miletich has identified most of the seminal articles related to depression in recent years. He has spared us, as readers, a summary of every article (such a book would be unmanageable) but has provided selective comments regarding publications throughout the **Sourcebook.**

Another value of this book is that John Miletich has called heavily upon book chapters and books for the general public. This approach may not be of a great value to investigators who are at the cutting edge of the field (they will wish for cutting edge information usually published in refereed journals). Nevertheless, there are many persons (undergraduate and undergraduate professional students in medicine, nursing, social work, and psychology as well as practitioners) who can benefit from this **Sourcebook** as a background for research papers or just for their own edification.

Certainly, some references are more important than others. Two I particularly call to the attention of the reader - 1.402 and 1.403, that is, the **Depression in Primary Care "Clinical Practice Guidelines" (Volumes 1 and 2).** Published practice guidelines are going to become much more important to practitioners in the future and the authors have attempted to distill the current literature into a structure for treating a variety of disorders, in this case, the depressive disorders. These guidelines are not algorithms that can be followed in cookbook fashion, but rather fill a role similar to a good travel guidebook, that is, providing direction without constraining the initiative of the traveler. This **Sourcebook,** in like manner, can serve as a guidebook to the extensive literature on depression.

Therefore, I would recommend this work to the general public as a useful reference to a complex subject. John Miletich has already compiled similar reviews in other areas and they have proven valuable and I anticipate this one to prove valuable as well.

Dan G. Blazer, M.D., Ph.D.
J.P. Gibbons Professor of Psychiatry
and Behavioral Sciences
Dean of Medical Education
Duke University Medical Center
Durham, North Carolina

PREFACE

Any one of the following may be a symptom of depression: sadness, crying, preoccupation with death, guilt, insomnia, change in appetite, fatigue, loss of interest in sex, or shame. But these nine symptoms - and others - are not limited to depression. Medication including nondrowsy decongestant can cause insomnia. Thyroid disease can bring about change in appetite. Anemia can cause fatigue. However, several or more of these symptoms - existing collectively in a person - most probably indicate depression.

Depression is an illness affecting approximately 100 million people worldwide, approximately 16 million people in the U.S. The word "depression" is derived from "deprimere," a Latin word meaning "to press down." Depressed persons feel "down," as if the weight of the world is on their shoulders.

Some elderly people use "melancholia" to indicate what many younger persons call "depression." Melancholia has been traced back more than 2,500 years to Ancient Greece and Rome, Hippocrates having attributed melancholia to black bile. Bodily fluids, at this time, were believed to account for personality. An excess of black bile indicated a melancholic (depressed) individual.

Depression literature reveals many expressions qualifying the meaning of depression. "Agitated," "covert," "nonpsychotic postpartum," "fatigue-debt," "self-pity," and "vital" are some of these expressions.

Depression, for the purposes of this book, includes not only popular notions of depression, but also Seasonal Affective Disorder (SAD) and bipolar depression, a newer term for manic depression. Readers interested in the specifics of word usage concerning depression should consult the latest edition of the **Diagnostic and Statistical Manual of Mental Disorders.**

Depression is not limited to a particular sex, race, age, occupation, or geographical region. Depression is universal - the common cold of mental illness - and is closely associated with suicide.

When White House aide Vincent Foster committed suicide in 1993, he was purportedly depressed. When rock star Kurt Cobain committed suicide in 1994, he also was depressed, as are 6 million young people in the U.S. The book **Prozac Nation: Young and Depressed in America** describes a young woman's depression since childhood and her life affected by prescription drugs.

There are in the U.S. approximately 30,000 suicides annually. Twice as many suicides may not be reported. At least 80% of suicides in Canada are related to depression. In Great Britain the Royal College of Psychiatrists began in 1992 a Defeat Depression Campaign. The economic costs of depression in the U.S. are $16 billion annually.

There is no single explanation for depression. The death of a loved one, the end of a close friendship, the failure of an investment - all losses - figure prominently in the psychoanalytic model of depression. The biomedical model attributes depression to imbalances in the brain of chemical substances, norepinephrine and serotonin. The behavioral view - its roots go back to the late 1920s - is that depression is caused by insufficient positive reinforcement. The cognitive model accounts for depression in terms of negative cognitions, and how depressed individuals view themselves, the world, and the future - the cognitive triad. The systems model incorporates psychoanalytic, biomedical, and other factors.

There is no single commonly accepted cause of depression and no single commonly accepted treatment. Amphetamines were used to treat depression as far back as 1936. Psychotherapy and electroconvulsive treatment (ECT) were used prior to the late 1950s. Then the tricyclic antidepressants and monoamine oxidase (MAO) inhibitors were developed. Behavioral and cognitive approaches were first used in the late 1960s and early 1970s. The selective serotonin reuptake inhibitors (SSRIs) are the drugs for depression in the 1990s. Of all the SSRIs, Prozac (Fluoxetine) has received the most attention in the popular press.

There are side effects associated with nonpharmacological and pharmacological methods of treatment. Confusion, impaired judgement, and amnesia occur in some patients treated with ECT. The tricyclic antidepressants cause drowsiness, dry mouth, and constipation. The MAO inhibitors can if combined with certain foods - cheese for example - cause a dramatic rise in blood pressure. Prozac is easier to tolerate than are the tricyclics, but diarrhea and inhibition of orgasm are among its side effects.

This book is a compilation of diverse information on depression in publications by approximately 200 publishers - and other sources - spanning nearly seven decades, 1927-1994. There is in these publications reference to earlier publications, such as Sigmund Freud's classic paper "Mourning and Melancholia" published in 1917, and Robert Burton's classic work **Anatomy of Melancholy** published in 1621.

The information is in many forms including: books, review papers, newsletters, databases, CD-ROM, television programs, and videocassettes.

This information is organized into five chapters, sixteen appendices, a list of acronyms, and separate author and subject indexes. The annotations are informational, but are not intended to be abstracts.

This book is intended for physicians, psychologists, nurses, social workers, suicidologists, and paramedics. It is also intended for students in these professions.

Librarians can use this volume to locate specific facts about depression and as a starting point for locating more detailed information. They can also use this book as a selection aid to acquire publications and other resources for their libraries.

Families and friends of depressed persons can use this volume to locate information which can help depressed persons out of their depression.

I am grateful to the following for their assistance: in Los Angeles, California: Los Angeles Center for Cognitive Therapy; in Washington, DC: American Psychiatric Association; in Honolulu, Hawaii: University of Hawaii (Manoa) Library; in Chicago, Illinois: American Medical Association and the National Depressive and Manic-Depressive Association; in Rockville, Maryland: the National Institute of Mental Health; in Great Neck, New York; Constance E. Lieber, National Alliance for Research on Schizophrenia and Depression; in New York, New York: The Foundation for Depression and Manic Depression, Inc. and the National Foundation for Depressive Illness, Inc.; in Durham, North Carolina, Dan G. Blazer and Erdman B. Palmore, Duke University Medical Center; in Morrisville, Pennsylvania: Trish Bukowski and Nancy Berchtold, Depression after Delivery; in Alexandria, Virginia: National Mental Health Association; in Calgary, Alberta: Calgary Public Library and the University of Calgary Library; in Edmonton, Alberta; Anna M. Duerr and Judy Molden, Alberta Health Community Health Section Library; Teresa Bendall and Betty Forster, Alberta Family and Social Services Library; Concordia College Library; Edmonton General Hospital Library; Edmonton Public Library; Glenrose Hospital Library; Grey Nun's Hospital Library; Sylvia Flood, Grant MacEwan Community College Library; Denise Holmen, Alberta Alcohol and Drug Abuse Commission Library; Misercordia Hospital Library; Royal Alenandra Hospital Library; Royal Alexandra Hospital School of Nursing Library; and the University of Alberta Library; in Old Chelsea, Quebec: Patricia Black, Canadian Psychological Association; in Kingston-Upon-Thames, Surrey, England: Brenda Fontain, Manic Depression Fellowship; in London, England: Simon James, The Association for Postnatal Illness; and in Dublin, Ireland: AWARE.

Thank you to Guy Perrotta, Assistant Production Editor.

I am especially grateful to Dr. James T. Sabin, Executive Vice President, Greenwood Publishing Group, for his advice and assistance.

ACRONYMS

AA	Alcoholics Anonymous
BDI	Beck Depression Inventory
CBC	Complete Blood Count
CDI	Children's Depression Inventory
CDS	Children's Depression Scale
CES-D	Center for Epidemiologic Studies Depression Scale
COPD	Chronic Obstructive Pulmonary Disease
CWD	Coping With Depression
DACL	Depression Adjective Checklist
DD	Dysthymic Disorder
DIS	Diagnostic Interview Schedule
DM	Dextromethorphan
DMST	Dexamethasone Suppression Test
DSRS	Depression Self-Rating Scale
ECT	Electroconvulsive Treatment/Therapy
EKG	Electrocardiogram
FCCL	Feelings and Concerns Checklist
FDA	Food and Drug Administration
GLAD	Graduated Linear Assessment of Delight
HRS	Hamilton Rating Scale
MAACL	Multiple Affect Adjective Check List
MAOI	Monoamine Oxidase Inhibitor
MDAMT	Manic-Depressive Association of Metropolitan Toronto
MDARP	Manic-Depressive Association for the Region of Peel
MMPI	Minnesota Multiphasic Personality Inventory
MMSE	Mini-Mental State Examination
MS	Multiple Sclerosis
NA	Narcotics Anonymous
NAFDI	National Foundation for Depressive Illness
NARSAD	National Alliance for Research on Schizophrenia and Depression
NAS	National Academy of Sciences
NIMH	National Institute of Mental Health
NRC	National Research Council
PCP	Phencyclidine
PMS	Premenstrual Syndrome
PMT	Premenstrual Tension
POMS	Profile of Mood States
POW	Prisoner of War
RA	Rheumatoid Arthritis
REM	Rapid Eye Movement

SAD	Seasonal Affective Disorder
	Systematic Assessment of Depression
SADS	Schedule for Affective Disorders and Schizophrenia
SDS	Self-Rating Depression Scale
SSRI	Selective Serotonin Reuptake Inhibitor
TDCRP	Treatment of Depression Collaborative Research Program
TM	Transcendental Meditation
UCLA	University of California Los Angeles
WPA	World Psychiatric Association
YGDS	Yesavage Geriatric Depression Scale

Chapter 1

DEFINITIONS, IDENTIFICATION, DIAGNOSIS

BOOKS FOR PROFESSIONALS AND THE GENERAL PUBLIC

1.001. Anthony, E. James and Therese Benedak. Editors. **Depression and Human Existence.** Boston, MA: Little, Brown and Company, 1975.

1.002. Attkisson, C. Clifford and Jane M. Zich. Editors. **Depression in Primary Care: Screening and Detection.** New York, NY: Routledge, 1990.

"Screening Procedures in Primary Care: History and Uses" (Paul S. Frame) and "Depression Screening Instruments: History and Issues" (Jane M. Murphy) are two of the papers which resulted from the Tiburon Conference held in June 1987. The conference was sponsored by the National Institute of Mental Health (NIMH) and the University of California, San Francisco.

1.003. Ayd, Frank J., Jr. **Recognizing the Depressed Patient: With Essentials of Management and Treatment.** New York, NY: Grune and Stratton, 1961.

1.004. Bailey, Linda J. **How to Get Going When You Can Barely Get Out of Bed.** Englewood Cliffs, NJ: Prentice-Hall, 1984.

Depression results when individuals forfeit their personal power. To overcome guilt, insecurity, and anxiety is to conquer frustration and to regain personal power.

1.005. Beck, Aaron T. **Depression: Clinical, Experimental, and Theoretical Aspects.** London: Staples, 1967.

1.006. Becker, Joseph. **Depression: Theory and Research.** Washington, DC: V.H. Winston and Sons, 1974.

1.007. Belle, Deborah. Editor. **Lives in Stress: Women and Depression.** Beverly Hills, CA: Sage, 1982.

Low-income mothers are at a high risk for depression. Unpredictable income, poor housing, dependence on social agencies, discrimination, and violent crime are some of the realities for many of these women. These women, furthermore, deal continuously with emergencies and feel they have little control over their lives. The foregoing information was obtained by The Stress and Families Project.

1.008. Belmaker, Robert H. and H.M. van Praag. Editors. **Mania: An Evolving Concept.** Jamaica, NY: Spectrum, 1980.

Thirty-five contributors question in twenty-three chapters long-held beliefs about mania. Lithium, for example, is not specific for manic-depressive illness. Treatment prognosis for mania is not, in actual fact, always excellant.

1.009. Billig, Nathan. **To Be Old and Sad: Understanding Depression in the Elderly.** Lexington, MA: Lexington Books, 1987.

1.010. Braiker, Harriet B. **Getting Up When You're Feeling Down: A Woman's Guide to Overcoming and Preventing Depression.** New York, NY: G.P. Putnam's Sons, 1988.

The Braiker Mood Scale for Women; Carroll Rating Scale; Blue Mood Questionnaire; Daily Mood Rating Form and Diary; and Rosenberg Self-esteem Scale are self-diagnostic measures of depressive illness. These and other self-administered research instruments, while of value, cannot equal or surpass the assessment available from a trained professional. This is the opinion of Dr. Harriet Braiker, clinical psychologist and director, Praxis Training Group.

1.011. Breslau, Lawrence D. and Marie R. Haug. Editors. **Depression and Aging: Causes, Care, and Consequences.** New York, NY: Springer, 1983.

Twenty-eight health sciences professionals from across the U.S. offer a variety of perspectives regarding diagnosis; causal factors; social and individual consequences; and other aspects of depression in the elderly.

1.012. Burns, David D. **Feeling Good: The New Mood Therapy.** New York, NY: Signet, 1980.

Cognitive therapy is a drug-free therapy developed at the University of Pennsylvania School of Medicine. The basic tenet of this therapy: moods can be altered, and depression cured, by changing how a person thinks. Building self-esteem and overcoming lethargy and procrastination are among the steps to be taken towards a cure.

1.013. Cameron, Oliver G. Editor. **Presentations of Depression: Depressive Symptoms in Medical and Other Psychiatric Disorders.** New York, NY: John Wiley and Sons, 1987.

1.014. Cappeliez, Philippe and Robert J. Flynn. Editors. **Depression and the Social Environment: Research and Intervention with Neglected Populations.** Montreal, PQ: McGill-Queen's University Press, 1993.

Canadian Native Indians; immigrants and refugees; and people with physical disabilities are three examples of populations which have been neglected regarding the study of depression.

1.015. Carlson, Richard. **You Can Feel Good Again: Common-Sense Therapy for Releasing Depression and Changing Your Life.** New York, NY: Dutton, 1993.

1.016. Carter, Sharon and Lawrence Clayton. **Coping with Depression.** New York, NY: Rosen, 1990.

1.017. Chiles, John. **Teenage Depression and Suicide.** New York, NY: Chelsea House Publishers, 1986.

1.018. Dalton, Katharina. **Depression after Childbirth: How to Recognize and Treat Postnatal Illness.** Oxford: Oxford University Press, 1980.

Dr. Katharina Dalton, who has studied postnatal depression for three decades, states this type of depression can range from a mild case of the blues to mental illness, lasting twenty years. Dr. Dalton, who has four children, contends a hormonal change is the cause of postnatal depression. The common belief is that sleeplessness and loss of independence, after the arrival of the baby, are among the causes. Hormone therapy has cured some women.

1.019. Davies, Brian, Bernard J. Carroll and Robert M. Mowbray. Editors. **Depressive Illness: Some Research Studies.** Springfield, IL: Charles C. Thomas, 1972.

Plasma cortisol levels; the Dexamethasone Suppression Test; and indoleamines and cerebrospinal fluid are three areas of depression research.

1.020. Degrassi Talks Depression. Toronto, ON: Boardwalk Books, 1992.

The book version of the television documentary **Degrassi Talks,** which is produced by Playing With Time Inc. The Canadian Broadcasting Corporation (CBC), Health and Welfare Canada, and Telefilm Canada also cooperate in the production of this TV series. Teenagers are the target audience of this series.

1.021. DePaulo, J. Raymond, Jr. and Keith Russell Ablow. **How to Cope with Depression: A Complete Guide for You and Your Family.** New York, NY: Fawcett Crest, 1989.

1.022. Depue, Richard A. Editor. **The Psychobiology of the Depressive Disorders: Implications for the Effects of Stress.** New York, NY: Academic Press, 1979.

1.023. Dominian, Jack. **Depression.** Revised Edition. n.p., Fontana/Collins, 1990.

1.024. Emery, Gary. **Getting Undepressed: How a Woman Can Change Her Life through Cognitive Therapy.** New York, NY: Simon and Schuster, 1988.

1.025. Enelow, Allen J. Editor. **Depression in Medical Practice.** West Point, PA: Merck Sharp and Dohme, 1970.

1.026. Fieve, Ronald R. **Moodswing.** Revised and Expanded Edition. New York, NY: Bantam Books, 1989.

Dr. Ronald R. Fieve, who pioneered the use of lithium for treating manic depression in the U.S., also established the Foundation for Depression and Manic Depression. Millions of Americans are afflicted with moodswing, which ranges from exhilaration to despair.

1.027. Flach, Frederic. Editor. **Affective Disorders,** Directions in Psychiatry Monograph Series, Number 3, New York, NY: W.W. Norton and Company, 1988.

1.028. Flach, Frederic F. **The Secret Strength of Depression.** New York, NY: Bantam Books, 1974.

1.029. Frankel, Lois P. **Women, Anger and Depression: Strategies for Self-Empowerment.** Deerfield Beach, FL: Health Communications, 1992.

1.030. Freden, Lars. **Psychosocial Aspects of Depression: No Way Out?** Chichester: John Wiley and Sons, 1982.

1.031. French, Alfred P. and Irving N. Berlin. Editors. **Depression in Children and Adolescents.** New York, NY: Human Sciences Press, 1979.

The twelve papers in this book resulted from a conference in Berkeley, California, June 11-12, 1976. Melvin Lewis, Irving Philips, Harold Boverman, and Charlotte Bible were some of the conference participants and authors.

1.032. Gallant, Donald M. and George M. Simpson. Editors. **Depression: Behavioral, Biochemical, Diagnostic and Treatment Concepts.** New York, NY: Spectrum, 1976.

1.033. Georgotas, Anastasios and Robert Cancro. Editors. **Depression and Mania.** New York, NY: Elsevier Science, 1988.

Fifty-four contributors discuss in forty-two chapters, divided into six parts, depression and mania. Five examples of chapters: (1) "Seasonal Affective Disorder" (Frederick M. Jacobsen and Norman E. Rosenthal); (2) "Psychoendocrinology of Depression and Mania" (Peter E. Stokes); (3) "Convulsive Therapy for Affective Disorders" (Max Fink); (4) "Grief and Mourning" (John E. Ruark and Thomas A. Gonda); and (5) "Laboratory Tests in Depression and Mania" (Emil F. Coccaro, Richard A. Friedman and Larry J. Siever).

1.034. Gillett, Richard. **Overcoming Depression.** Toronto, ON: Macmillan of Canada, 1987.

Dr. Richard Gillett has in his book diagnostic questionnaires which supplement orthodox, alternative, and self-help methods of treating depression. He admits having experienced the blues and inhibition. Hypnosis, meditation, psychodrama, and Gestalt are some of the treatment methods he has used.

1.035. Gold, Mark S. and Lois B. Morris. **The Good News about Depression: Cures and Treatments in the New Age of Psychiatry.** New York, NY: Bantam Books, 1988.

Approximately 100 million people worldwide suffer from severe biological depression, which requires a doctor's care. The number for the U.S. may be 16 million persons. Hundreds of thousands of other individuals experience a depression which does not have overt symptoms - masked depression. Biopsychiatry, that is, medical psychiatry, is psychiatry based on the medical model and, by utilizing the latest scientific advances, can effectively treat depression.

1.036. Gotlib, Ian H. and Catherine A. Colby. **Treatment of Depression: An Interpersonal Systems Approach.** New York, NY: Pergamon, 1987.

Depressed patients can be assessed and treated with the aid of a systems description of depression. This assertion is based on a view of depression as an interpersonal phenomenon. The marital and family relationships of depressed persons merit close study.

1.037. Greist, John H. and James W. Jefferson. **Depression and Its Treatment.** New, Revised Edition. New York, NY: Warner Books, 1992.

Dr. R.P. Snaith was instrumental in the development, at the Wakefield Hospital in 1971, of the Wakefield Self-Report Questionnaire. This questionnaire consists of twelve simple questions, which depressed persons answer to obtain a depression rating score. The person chooses one of four digits - 0 to 3 - in response to each question. Zero represents "No, not at all." Three represents "Yes, definitely." The first item on the questionnaire, for example, is: "I feel miserable and sad."

1.038. Halbreich, Uriel. Editor. **Hormones and Depression.** New York, NY: Raven, 1987.

Psychoneuroendocrinology, also known as behavioral endocrinology, may explain relationships between mood and behavioral symptoms and endocrine abnormalities. Hormones may be used as psychotropic drugs, if research indicates that hormones are a factor in maintaining balanced brain circuitry. Presently, however, most studies are animal studies. Fritz A. Henn has written about self-helplessness and melancholia in animals.

1.039. Hammen, Constance. **Depression Runs in Families: The Social Context of Risk and Resilience in Children of Depressed Mothers.** New York, NY: Springer-Verlag, 1991.

Questionnaires, reports, school records, and observations - in addition to approximately 1,000 interviews - form the basis of the UCLA Family Stress Project, the forerunner of **Depression Runs in Families: The Social Context of Risk and Resilience in Children of Depressed Mothers.**

1.040. Hazleton, Lesley. **The Right to Feel Bad: Coming to Terms with Normal Depression.** Garden City, NY: Dial Press, 1984.

1.041. Hinchliffe, Mary K., Douglas Hooper and F. John Roberts. **The Melancholy Marriage: Depression in Marriage and Psychosocial Approaches to Therapy.** Chichester: John Wiley and Sons, 1978.

1.042. Jack, Dana Crowley. **Silencing the Self: Women and Depression.** Cambridge, MA: Harvard University Press, 1991.

The Silencing the Self Scale consists of thirty-one statements. A woman has five options from which to choose, regarding each statement, ranging from "strongly disagree" (statement 1) to "strongly agree" (statement 5). She must circle one of five numbers - 1, 2, 3, 4, 5 - pertaining to each statement. Selfishness, independence, and anger are a few of the concepts evaluated by this scale.

1.043. Jackson, Stanley W. **Melancholia and Depression: From Hippocratic Times to Modern Times.** New Haven, CT: Yale University Press, 1986.

Feelings of dejection and sadness existed long before the word depression was used to refer to these feelings or states. These feelings were, for many centuries, referred to as melancholia. Melancholia has been traced back in time over 2,500 years to Ancient Greece and Rome. Lycanthropy and nostalgia are two variants of melancholia.

1.044. Jacobson, Edith. **Depression: Comparative Studies of Normal, Neurotic, and Psychotic Conditions.** New York, NY: International Universities Press, 1971.

1.045. Kendall-Tackett, Kathleen A. and Glenda Kaufman Kantor. **Postpartum Depression: A Comprehensive Approach for Nurses.** Newbury Park, CA: Sage, 1993.

1.046. Kendell, R.E. **The Classification of Depressive Illnesses,** Institute of Psychiatry Maudsley Monographs, Number 18, London: Oxford University Press, 1968.

1.047. Kerns, Lawrence L. and Adrienne B. Lieberman. **Helping Your Depressed Child: A Reassuring Guide to the Causes and Treatments of Childhood and Adolescent Depression.** Rocklin, CA: Prima, 1993.

Ten percent of the children and adolescents in the U.S. are seriously depressed. Six million young persons are afflicted with depression, a potentially fatal psychiatric illness. Childhood depression is the area of specialization for Dr. Kerns through his affiliation with the University of Illinois and the Institute for Juvenile Research.

1.048. Kiev, Ari. **Riding through the Downers, Hassles, Snags and Funks.** New York, NY: E.P. Dutton, 1980.

Dr. Ari Kiev, psychiatrist, expert consultant, and founder of Life Strategy Workshops, has written his eighty-five page book as if he has written a long letter. His target audience are young people. Dr. Kiev's message: depressed persons should delay their responses to pressures. School, friends, and parents are the usual sources of pressures and demands. Only when people have a realistic idea of their needs and desires can these people master their own behavior.

1.049. Kiev, Ari. Editor. **Somatic Manifestations of Depressive Disorders.** Amsterdam: Excerpta Medica, 1974.

1.050. Klein, Donald F. and Paul H. Wender. **Do You Have a Depressive Illness?: How to Tell, What to Do.** New York, NY: New American Library, 1988.

1.051. Kline, Nathan S. Editor. **Factors in Depression.** New York, NY: Raven, 1974.

1.052. Lee, Essie E. and Richard Wortman. **Down Is Not Out: Teenagers and Depression.** New York, NY: Julian Messner, 1986.

1.053. Lesse, Stanley. Editor. **Masked Depression.** New York, NY: Jason Aronson, 1974.

Dr. Lesse's training in neurology and psychiatry brought him into contact with patients whose complaints were hypochondriacal or psychosomatic. These complaints masked an underlying depression. He learned, when he studied patients in their forties, fifties, and sixties, that at least 50% of these patients had variations of masked depression. Dr. Lesse discovered that alcoholism, bulimia, and impotence were only a few conditions masking depression. Over 40% of his patients with this problem had suicidal ideation. Masked depression, although occurring frequently, usually takes years to recognize.

1.054. Lin, Nan, Alfred Dean and Walter M. Ensel. Editors. **Social Support, Life Events and Depression.** Orlando, FL: Academic Press, 1986.

1.055. Mahendra, B. **Depression: The Disorder and Its Associations.** Lancaster: MTP Press, 1987.

1.056. Mann, J. John. Editor. **Models of Depressive Disorders: Psychological, Biological, and Genetic Perspectives,** The Depressive Illness Series, Volume 2, New York, NY: Plenum, 1989.

Cognitive, intrapsychic, animal, and neurobiological models are some of the models which have been formulated to account for depressive disorders.

1.057. Maser, Jack D. Editor. **Depression and Expressive Behavior.** Hillsdale, NJ: Lawrence Erlbaum Associates, 1987.

Body movements, facial behavior, vocal assessment, and the pacing of speech have been researched in order to better understand affective disorders. Allen T. Dittmann, Paul Ekman, Klaus R. Scherer, and Aron W. Siegman are examples of individuals who have done this type of research.

1.058. McCann, C. Douglas and Norman S. Endler. Editors. **Depression: New Directions in Theory, Research, and Practice.** Toronto, ON: Wall and Emerson, 1990.

Four factors in depression - psychosocial, psychological, psychobiological, biological - and an example of a paper about each factor: (1) psychosocial, "Sociopolitical

Factors and Stigma in Depression" (Norman S. Endler); (2) psychological, "Are Cognitive Approaches to Depression Useful?" (Nicholas A. Kuiper, L. Joan Olinger and Rod A. Martin); (3) psychobiological, "Treatment-Resistant Depression and Rapid Cycling Affective Disorder" (Emmanuel Persad); and (4) biological, "The Role of ECT in the Treatment of Depression" (Donald P. Hay and Linda K. Hay).

1.059. McGrath, Ellen. **When Feeling Bad Is Good.** New York, NY: Henry Holt and Company, 1992.

1.060. Mendels, Joseph. **Concepts of Depression.** New York, NY: John Wiley and Sons, 1970.

1.061. Mitchell, Ross. **Depression.** Harmondsworth: Penguin, 1975.

Depression is viewed as a mood, experience, attitude to life, and illness. Early infancy, grief, life crises, suicidal behavior, sex, and alcohol are related to depression. Drugs, electroconvulsive therapy (ECT), leucotomy, and hospitalization aid in managing depression. Eight case histories help explain depression. Over two dozen photographs. 2 cartoon illustrations. 3 diagrams. 18 references.

1.062. Mondimore, Francis Mark. **Depression: The Mood Disease.** Baltimore, MD: Johns Hopkins University Press, 1990.

1.063. Morrison, Helen L. Editor. **Children of Depressed Parents: Risk, Identification, and Intervention.** New York, NY: Grune and Stratton, 1983.

1.064. Oppenheim, Janet. **"Shattered Nerves": Doctors, Patients, and Depression in Victorian England.** New York, NY: Oxford University Press, 1991.

1.065. Ostow, Mortimer. **The Psychology of Melancholy.** New York, NY: Harper and Row, 1970.

1.066. Papolos, Demitri F. and Janice Papolos. **Overcoming Depression.** New York, NY: Harper and Row, 1988.

A copy of the Affective Disorders Questionnaire, consisting of forty-nine questions, is reproduced on pages 247-249.

1.067. Paykel, Eugene S. Editor. **Handbook of Affective Disorders.** Second Edition. New York, NY: Guilford Press, 1992.

Information about affective disorders is organized into five categories and one of a number of examples for each category is included: (1) descriptive aspects (symptoms); (2) causative aspects (epidemiological); (3) medication and physical treatments (ECT); (4) psychotherapeutic, cognitive, and social treatments (cognitive therapy); and (5) special aspects (transcultural).

1.068. Podell, Ronald M. **Contagious Emotions: Staying Well When Your Loved One Is Depressed.** New York, NY: Pocket Books, 1992.

1.069. Preston, John. **You Can Beat Depression: A Guide to Recovery.** San Luis Obispo, CA: Impact, 1989.

Clinical psychologist Dr. John Preston managed the Depression Clinic at Kaiser Permanente Medical Center in Sacramento, California. He has to his credit numerous publications in neuropsychology and several audiocassettes.

1.070. Priest, Robert. **Anxiety and Depression: A Practical Guide to Recovery.** Scarborough, ON: Prentice-Hall Canada, 1983.

In a survey of depressed women, some of the findings were: (1) 76% of those surveyed reported crying easily; (2) 76% indicated feeling lethargic; (3) 73% experienced loss of concentration; and (4) 66% reported being absent-minded.

1.071. Pyszczynski, Tom and Jeff Greenberg. **Hanging On and Letting Go: Understanding the Onset, Progression, and Remission of Depression.** New York, NY: Springer-Verlag, 1992.

Depression is caused, in part, by certain life goals which become unfeasible, but which a person cannot abandon, this resulting in reflection upon lost goals. To gradually abandon these goals and to work towards other goals is to overcome the depression.

1.072. Racagni, Giorgio and Enrico Smeraldi. Editors. **Anxious Depression: Assessment and Treatment.** New York, NY: Raven, 1987.

During September 22-23, 1986, in Milan, Italy, participants met at a workshop to discuss anxious depression. This book consisting of twenty-six papers by sixty-five contributors is based on the workshop. Psychopathology, family history, biology, and treatment are covered.

1.073. Rippere, Vicky and Ruth Williams. Editors. **Wounded Healers: Mental Health Workers' Experiences of Depression.** Chichester: John Wiley and Sons, 1985.

Mental health workers from England, Australia, Canada, and other countries share, in nineteen personal essays, their accounts of having been depressed. Psychiatry, clinical psychology, and occupational therapy are some of the professions these workers represent. One of the contributors, Margaret, a general practitioner in Scotland, committed suicide, after sixteen years of recurrent depression.

1.074. Robbins, Paul R. **Understanding Depression.** Jefferson, NC: McFarland and Company, 1993.

1.075. Rosellini, Gayle and Mark Worden. **Here Comes the Sun: Dealing with Depression.** Center City, MN: Hazelden, 1987.

1.076. Rush, John. **Beating Depression.** New York, NY: Facts on File, 1983.

Virginia Ironside, who wrote the introduction, experienced depression for years, wishing she were dead. She states that a depressed person and depression are not one, that is, the same thing. Depression is a condition and is not intrinsically the person whom the depression affects. Cognitive therapy can be used to treat depression. A depressed person can, through this therapy, build confidence, after unlearning negative ways of thinking.

1.077. Schwartz, Arthur and Ruth M. Schwartz. **Depression: Theories and Treatments: Psychological, Biological, and Social Perspectives.** New York, NY: Columbia University Press, 1993.

1.078. Seligman, Martin E.P. **Helplessness: On Depression, Development, and Death.** San Francisco, CA: W.H. Freeman and Company, 1975.

Dr. Martin Seligman began research on learned helplessness in 1964, believing that anxiety and depression evolve from a feeling of helplessness, which is learned. Depression dissipates when depressed persons increase control over their environment. Children may be "immunized" against depression for life, if they can be taught to exert control over certain aspects of their environment. Sudden unexpected death in old age homes, POW (prisoner of war) camps, zoos, and elsewhere can be related to helplessness.

1.079. Shamoo, Tonia K. and Philip G. Patros. **"I Want to Kill Myself": Helping Your Child Cope with Depression and Suicidal Thoughts.** Lexington, MA: D.C. Heath and Company, 1990.

1.080. Silverstein, Herma. **Teenage Depression.** New York, NY: Franklin Watts, 1990.

1.081. Smyth, Angela. **Seasonal Affective Disorder.** London: Thorsons, 1991.

The onset of Seasonal Affective Disorder (SAD) is in the fall. There is relief in summer, with SAD recurring annually. There is no seasonal pattern in classical depression. The SAD sufferer tends to sleep and eat more. The person experiencing classical depression has difficulty sleeping and experiences a loss of appetite. The SAD person gains weight; the classically depressed person either loses weight or the weight does not change. While the mood of the SAD individual is influenced by changes in latitude and/or the number of hours of daylight, the mood of the depressed person is not influenced by these changes.

1.082. Stefanis, C.N. Editor. **Recent Advances in Depression.** Oxford: Pergamon, 1983.

Depression and suicide are closely related. Approximately 150 million people worldwide exhibit symptoms of clnical depression. Suicide is under-reported. The number of deaths in Europe, officially registered as suicide, is approximately 100,000 annually. However, over a thousand individuals commit suicide daily. All this contributes, perhaps immeasurably, to socioeconomic and other problems.

1.083. Sutherland Learning Associates. **Depression Today: Confident Clinical Office Management, Part One: Recognizing and Diagnosing Depression.** New York, NY: C.M.E. Communications, 1978.

1.084. Thompson, C. and T. Silverstone. Editors. **Seasonal**

Affective Disorder. London: CNS (Clinical Neuroscience), 1989.

Depression (usually in winter), increased desire for sweet-tasting carbohydrates (with consequent weight gain), and hypersomnia characterize Seasonal Affective Disorder (SAD).

1.085. Tsuang, Ming T. and Stephen V. Faraone. **The Genetics of Mood Disorders.** Baltimore, MD: Johns Hopkins University Press, 1990.

1.086. Whitlock, F.A. **Symptomatic Affective Disorders: A Study of Depression and Mania Associated with Physical Disease and Medication,** Personality and Psychopathology, Number 31, Sydney, NSW: Academic Press, 1982.

1.087. Whybrow, Peter and Robert Bahr. **The Hibernation Response: Why You Feel Fat, Miserable, and Depressed from October through March - and How You Can Cheer Up through Those Dark Days of Winter.** New York, NY: William Morrow and Company, 1988.

1.088. Whybrow, Peter C., Hagop S. Akiskal and William T. McKinney, Jr. **Mood Disorders: Toward a New Psychobiology.** New York, NY: Plenum, 1984.

Adolf Meyer was the first person to use the term psychobiology, indicating there are psychosocial and biological factors in psychobiology.

1.089. Williams, Richard and J. Thomas Dalby. Editors. **Depression in Schizophrenics.** New York, NY: Plenum, 1989.

A World Psychiatric Association Symposium on Depression in Schizophrenics was held in Calgary, Alberta, July 6-7, 1988. Theoretical aspects; phenomenology; suicide and prognosis in schizophrenics with depression; and treatment of depression in schizophrenics were the four main areas addressed by the symposium participants.

1.090. Willner, Paul. **Depression: A Psychobiological Synthesis.** New York, NY: John Wiley and Sons, 1985.

1.091. Wolman, Benjamin B. and George Stricker. Editors. **Depressive Disorders: Facts, Theories, and Treatment Methods.** New York, NY: John Wiley and Sons, 1990.

One hundred million people throughout the world are diagnosed annually as suffering from depression. The ratio of depressive disorders to schizophrenia is ten to one. There is considerable diversity of opinion regarding, for example, the etiology and treatment methods of depressive disorders, let alone other aspects. In fact, between 1952 and 1987, each new edition of the **Diagnostic and Statistical Manual of Mental Disorders** contained new data pertaining to facts, concepts, approaches.

1.092. Wolpert, Edward A. Editor. **Manic-Depressive Illness: History of a Syndrome.** New York, NY: International Universities Press, 1977.

To understand the history of manic-depressive illness, it is essential to first note pertinent classic papers. Examples include: (1) "Notes on the Psycho-Analytical Investigation and Treatment of Manic-Depressive Insanity and Allied Conditions" (Karl Abraham, 1912); (2) "Mourning and Melancholia" (Sigmund Freud, 1917); (3) "Manic-Depressive Insanity" (Emil Kraepelin, 1921); (4) "Intensive Psychotherapy of Manic-Depressives" (Frieda Fromm-Reichmann, 1949); (5) "Contribution to the Metapsychology of Cyclothymic Depression" (Edith Jacobson, 1953); (6) "Family History Studies: The Genetics of Mania" Theodore Reich, Paula J. Clayton and George Winokur, 1969); and (7) "Juvenile Manic-Depressive Illness: Clinical and Therapeutic Considerations" (Sherman C. Feinstein and Edward A. Wolpert, 1973).

1.093. Yapko, Michael D. **Free Yourself from Depression.** Emmaus, PA: Rodale, 1992.

CHAPTERS AND SECTIONS IN BOOKS FOR PROFESSIONALS AND THE GENERAL PUBLIC

1.094. Action on Women's Addictions - Research and Education. "Women and Depression." in **Drug Wise: A Book for Older Women about Safe Drug Use**, by Action on Women's Addictions - Research and Education, 20-26. Kingston, ON: Aware Press, 1992.

1.095. Aldridge-Smith, Jan. "Depression." in **Lecture Notes on Behavioural Sciences**, edited by A.C.P. Sims and W.I. Hume, 154. Oxford: Blackwell Scientific, 1984.

1.096. Al-Issa, Ihsan. "Women and Depression." Chapter in **The Psychopathology of Women**, by Ihsan Al-Issa, 100-127.

Englewood Cliffs, NJ: Prentice-Hall, 1980.

1.097. Alloy, Lauren B., Lyn Y. Abramson and Debra A. Kossman. "The Judgment of Predictability in Depressed and Nondepressed College Students." Chapter in **Affect, Conditioning, and Cognition: Essays on the Determinants of Behavior,** edited by F. Robert Brush and J. Bruce Overmier, 229-246. Hillsdale, NJ: Lawrence Erlbaum Associates, 1985.

1.098. Anderson, Luleen S. "Understanding and Working with the Depressed, Suicidal Adolescent." Chapter in **New Directions for Counseling and Human Development,** edited by Richard Hayes and Roger Aubrey, 119-135. Denver, CO: Love, 1988.

Reasons for adolescent depression: (1) body chemistry changes; (2) intensified introspection; (3) heightened sexuality; and (4) gaining independence from parents and accompanying mourning. Reasons for adolescent suicide: (1) loss of a loved one; (2) loss of self-esteem; (3) shame; (4) rage; and (5) guilt. The likely motivation for suicide in adolescent females relates to interpersonal relationships; the likely motivation for adolescent males relates to performance issues, for example, pressure to succeed. Adolescents at-risk for suicide: (1) loners with few or no friends and poor social skills; (2) drug and alcohol abusers; (3) those who have great difficulty coping with a trauma, for example, a sudden loss; and (4) psychotics. 36 references. Author biographical information.

1.099. Andreasen, N.J.C., Russell Noyes, Jr. and C.E. Hartford. "Severe Depression." in **Stress and Coping: An Anthology,** edited by Alan Monat and Richard S. Lazarus, 223-224. New York, NY: Columbia University Press, 1977.

Six burn-injury patients - four from disturbed family backgrounds - developed severe depression, symptoms lasting longer than a week. Crying spells, decreased appetite, and insomnia were some of the symptoms. There were also guilt feelings about the disturbed family backgrounds.

1.100. Aneshensel, Carol S. "Marital and Employment Role-Strain, Social Support, and Depression among Adult Women." Chapter in **Stress, Social Support, and Women,** edited by Stevan E. Hobfoll, 99-114. Washington, DC: Hemisphere, 1986.

1.101. Anisman, Hymie. "Depression." in **Psychopharmacology of Aversively Motivated Behavior,** edited by Hymie

Anisman and Giorgio Bignami, 155-158. New York, NY: Plenum, 1978.

1.102. Anyan, Walter R., Jr. "Depression and Suicidal Behavior in Adolescence." Chapter in **Adolescent Medicine in Primary Care,** by Walter R. Anyan, Jr., 358-374. New York, NY: John Wiley and Sons, 1978.

1.103. Appelbaum, Stephen A. "Depression." in **The Anatomy of Change: A Menninger Foundation Report on Testing the Effects of Psychotherapy,** by Stephen A. Appelbaum, 143-149. New York, NY: Plenum, 1977.

1.104. Argyle, Michael and Mark Cook. "Depression." in **Gaze and Mutual Gaze,** by Michael Argyle and Mark Cook, 137-138. Cambridge: Cambridge University Press, 1976.

The types of people who gaze less are people with low self-esteem and those who are deceptive. Possible reasons why depressives look less: they avoid social contact and experience shame and guilt. 1 table.

1.105. Arieti, Silvano. "Depression." in **The Intrapsychic Self: Feeling, Cognition, and Creativity in Health and Mental Illness,** by Silvano Arieti, 116-117. New York, NY: Basic Books, 1967.

1.106. Arieti, Silvano. "Manic-Depressive Psychosis." in **The Intrapsychic Self: Feeling, Cognition, and Reativity in Health and Mental Illness,** by Silvano Arieti, 293-298. New York, NY: Basic Books, 1967.

1.107. Balint, Michael. "New Beginning and the Paranoid and the Depressive Syndromes." Chapter in **Primary Love and Psycho-Analytic Technique,** by Michael Balint, 230-249. New York, NY: Liveright, 1965.

1.108. Ban, Thomas A. "Manic-Depressive Psychosis." in **Conditioning and Psychiatry,** by Thomas A. Ban, 134-135. Chicago, IL: Aldine, 1964.

1.109. Ban, Thomas A. "Neurotic Depressions." in **Conditioning and Psychiatry,** by Thomas A. Ban, 74. Chicago, IL: Aldine, 1964.

The word "melancholia," referring to black bile, is attributed to Hippocrates. Neurotic depression, according to Pavlov, results from changes in the customary mode of living. This mode is based physiologically on dynamic stereotypes. A normal, healthy person can promptly establish a new dynamic stereotype. Certain neurotics require prolonged time to establish the stereotype. Anxiety and depression result from the delay.

1.110. Bartlett, Steven J. "Mood Disturbances (Affective Disorders)." in **When You Don't Know Where to Turn: A Self-Diagnosing Guide to Counseling and Therapy,** by Steven J. Bartlett, 73-74. Chicago, IL: Contemporary Books, 1987.

1.111. Beck, Aaron T. and Brian F. Shaw. "Cognitive Approaches to Depression." Chapter in **Handbook of Rational-Emotive Therapy,** by Albert Ellis and Russell Grieger, 119-134. New York, NY: Springer, 1977.

1.112. Bedi, Ashok R. "Cyclothymic Disorder." in **Alcohol and Drug Abuse Handbook,** edited by Roland E. Hernington, George R. Jacobson and David G. Benzer, 362-363. St. Louis, MO: Warren H. Green, 1987.

1.113. Bell, Ruth and Leni Zeiger Wildflower. "What Are the Symptoms of Serious Depression?" in **Talking with Your Teenager: A Book for Parents,** by Ruth Bell and Leni Zeiger Wildflower, 53-55. New York, NY: Random House, 1983.

1.114. Benedek, Therese. "Toward the Biology of the Depressive Constellation." Chapter in **Psychoanalytic Investigations: Selected Papers,** by Therese Benedek, 356-376. New York, NY: Quandrangle/The New York Times Book Co., 1973.

1.115. Bernstein, Lewis, Rosalyn S. Bernstein and Richard H. Dana. "Reactions of Depression and Loss of Self-Esteem to Illness and Treatment." in **Interviewing: A Guide for Health Professionals,** Second Edition, by Lewis Bernstein, Rosalyn S. Bernstein and Richard H. Dana, 149-153. New York, NY: Appleton-Century-Crofts, 1974.

1.116. Berzonsky, Michael D. "Depression in Adolescence." in **Adolescent Development,** by Michael D. Berzonsky, 503-504. New York, NY: Macmillan, 1981.

1.117. Blazer, Dan. "Depression." Chapter in **Principles of Geriatric Medicine and Gerontology,** Second Edition, by William R. Hazzard, Reubin Andres, Edwin L. Bierman and John P. Blass, 1010-1018. New York, NY: McGraw-Hill, 1990.

Three severity rating scales used to evaluate depression in late life: (1) Hamilton Depression Rating Scale, (2) Montgomery-Asberg Depression Rating Scale, and (3) Global Assessment Scale. Psychotherapy, pharmacotherapy, electroconvulsive therapy (ECT), and family therapy should be used to clinically manage depression in late life. 4 tables. 33 references.

1.118. Blazer, Dan. "Depression: Treatability of Psychopathology in Late Life." in **Clinical Geriatrics,** Third Edition, edited by Isadore Rossman, 596-599. Philadelphia, PA: J.B. Lippincott, 1986.

Irritability and agitation, rather than jovial mood, characterize manic episodes in late life. 1 table.

1.119. Blechman, Elaine A. "Social Learning Theories of Depression." in **Behavior Modification with Women,** edited by Elaine A. Blechman, 18-20. New York, NY: Guilford Press, 1984.

1.120. Bloomfield, Harold H. and Robert B. Kory. "Depression." in **Happiness: The TM Program, Psychiatry, and Enlightenment,** by Harold H. Bloomfield and Robert B. Kory, 167-172. New York, NY: Pocket Books, 1977.

Insomnia, early morning awakening, compulsive overeating, and bodily aches with no organic basis are a few somatic symptoms of depression. Most depressions do not last indefinitely. Repressed rage and negative reinforcement are viewed as causes of depression. TM (Transcendental Meditation) helps eliminate fatigue which sustains depression.

1.121. Blume, E. Sue. "When Memories Cripple: Depression." in **Secret Survivors: Uncovering Incest and Its Aftereffects in Women,** by E. Sue Blume, 88-90. New York, NY: John Wiley and Sons, 1990.

1.122. Blume, Judy. "Depression." in **Letters to Judy: What Your Kids Wish They Could Tell You,** by Judy Blume, 245-250. New York, NY: G.P. Putnam's Sons, 1986.

The loss of a boyfriend or girlfriend; alcohol or drug problem; death of a family member; or inability to effectively communicate with parents can lead to teenage depression. Includes six letters from teenagers to the author.

1.123. Bohm, Ewald. "The Depressions." Chapter in **A Textbook in Rorschach Test Diagnosis for Psychologists, Physicians and Teachers,** translated by Anne G. Beck and Samuel J. Beck, 253-267. New York, NY: Grune and Stratton, 1958.

1.124. Bosselman, Beulah Chamberlain. "Neurotic Depression." in **The Troubled Mind: A Psychiatric Study of Success and Failure in Human Adaptation,** by Beulah Chamberlain Bosselman, 107-109. New York, NY: Ronald Press, 1953.

The psychotic, unlike the neurotic, distorts reality to fit his or her mood. Psychotic depression appears to differ in degree only from neurotic depression. The latter is often transient and spontaneously clears up.

1.125. Brooks-Gunn, Jeanne. "Depressive Symptomatology." in **Adolescent Stress: Causes and Consequences,** edited by Mary Ellen Colten and Susan Gore, 139-140. New York, NY: Aldine de Gruyter, 1991.

1.126. Brooks-Gunn, Jeanne. "Mood Lability." in **Adolescent Stress: Causes and Consequences,** edited by Mary Ellen Colten and Susan Gore, 140. New York, NY: Aldine de Gruyter, 1991.

1.127. Bruno, Frank J. "Depressive Neurosis." in **Human Adjustment and Personal Growth: Seven Pathways,** by Frank J. Bruno, 13. New York, NY: John Wiley and Sons, 1977.

1.128. Bull, Peter. "Depression." in **Body Movement and Interpersonal Communication,** by Peter Bull, 88-89. Chichester: John Wiley and Sons, 1983.

Research in Canada, the U.S., and United Kingdom indicates the presence of depression in a person is communicated through bodily cues.

1.129. Burstein, Alvin G. "The Tearful, Depressed Patient." Chapter in **Psychosocial Basis of Medical Practice: An Introduction to Human Behavior,** Second Edition, 76-85. Baltimore, MD: Williams and Wilkins, 1979.

Many pathological depressions are caused by environmental pressures or internal fears, which inhibit the resolution of normal grieving processes. The depression scale is the scale most often elevated, when physically ill patients are administered the Minnesota Multiphasic Personality Inventory (MMPI). A person living alone - at a hotel, for example - is more likely to commit suicide than a person who lives with others and interacts socially with them. 4 references.

1.130. Butler, Pamela. "Depression: The Consequence of Helplessness." in **Self-Assertion for Women,** New Edition, by Pamela Butler, 28-30. San Francisco, CA: Harper and Row, 1981.

According to Martin Seligman, depression arises in women when they cannot, or appear to be unable to, control what happens to them. Many widowed or divorced women are, for this reason, depressed. They have lived for and through their husbands. Lynn Caine, in writing about widows, states that a woman whose husband dies is left without an identity she can call her own. Her husband, while he was alive, validated her existence. She without him is empty, incomplete, depressed.

1.131. Cahalan, Don, Ira H. Cisin and Helen M. Crossley. "Activities to Relieve Depression or Nervousness." in **American Drinking Practices: A National Study of Drinking Behavior and Attitudes,** by Don Cahalan, Ira H. Cisin and Helen M. Crossley, 149-152. New Brunswick, NJ: Rutgers Center of Alcohol Studies, 1969.

A table, Table 90, compares men and women in terms of abstainers and types of drinkers - infrequent, light, moderate, heavy - and relates this information to activities men and women engage in when the subjects are depressed or nervous.

1.132. Cain, Harvey D. "Depression and Suicidal Ideation." in **Flint's Emergency Treatment and Management,** Seventh Edition, by Harvey D. Cain, 619-620. Philadelphia, PA: W.B. Saunders, 1985.

The depressed individual engages in behavior which leads to less gratification, followed by more stress, followed by more depression. An increase in alcohol consumption, reduction of exercise, and altered appetite patterns are three examples of this behavior. This person must be asked clear and direct questions about intention to commit suicide. Exercise, good nutrition, supplemental vitamins, and family support should be used to help this depressed individual.

1.133. Cammer, Leonard. "Depression." in **Freedom from Compulsion: How to Liberate Yourself from the Uptight, Obsessive Patterns of Living that Rob You of Peace of Mind**, by Leonard Cammer, 135-140. New York, NY: Pocket Books, 1977.

1.134. Campbell, Ian M. "Depression." in **Clinical Applications of Rational-Emotive Therapy,** edited by Albert Ellis and Michael E. Bernard, 169. New York, NY: Plenum, 1985.

1.135. Campbell, Ross. "Why Teens Get Depressed." in **Parents and Teenagers,** by Jay Kesler, 201-202. Wheaton, IL: Victor Books, 1984.

Lack of concentration, daydreaming, increasingly shorter attention span, deep-rooted boredom, headaches, eating too much or too little, and lack of energy are indicators that a teenager may be depressed.

1.136. Carroll, Marilyn. "PCP and Depression." in **PCP: The Dangerous Angel**, by Marilyn Carroll, 60-61. New York, NY: Chelsea House Publishers, 1985.

Phencyclidine (PCP)-induced depression is most frequent among regular users of this drug. Depression rarely afflicts occasional users. Depression often follows acute toxicity or psychosis and can last several days or months. There is, at this time, a high risk of suicide and of relapse to continued use. Hospitalization is usually required because outpatients fail to regularly attend therapy or to take antidepressant medication. 1 photograph.

1.137. Cassem, Ned H. and Arthur J. Barsky. "Depressive Disorders." in **Massachusetts General Hospital Handbook of General Hospital Psychiatry**, Third Edition, edited by Ned H. Cassem, 132-133. St. Louis, MO: Mosby Year Book, 1991.

Aches, pains, and dizziness are common in depressed patients. These patients feel they are not worth treating, do not deserve to feel better, and feel hopeless about their condition improving. It appears that in depressed patients, the older the patient, the greater the number of hypochondriacal preoccupations.

1.138. Chafetz, Morris. "Why Do I Get More Depressed If I Drink?" in **Why Drinking Can Be Good for You**, by Morris Chafetz, 60. New York, NY: Stein and Day, 1976.

1.139. Chase, Cynthia. "Depression." in **Manual of Emergency Pediatrics,** Third Edition, by Robert M. Reece, 258-259. Philadelphia, PA: W.B. Saunders, 1984.

A depressed child, unlike a depressed adult, will be less direct in expressing feelings concerning depression. The child will use negativism or physical complaints to mask feelings. School performance will usually suffer. Depression may be alleviated by increasing family emotional support and brief outpatient follow-up. It may be necessary to hospitalize suicidal patients or those with severely impaired functioning.

1.140. Christie-Seely, Janet. "Depression." in **Working with the Family in Primary Care: A Systems Approach to Health and Illness,** edited by Janet Christie-Seely, 400-408. New York, NY: Praeger, 1984.

Many causes of depression have been advocated. Sociologists have associated depression with loss of role status, existentialists have attributed depression to loss of meaning in existence, and geneticists have linked depression to genetic vulnerability. 1 figure.

1.141. Ciolino, Charles. "Substance Abuse and Mood Disorders." Chapter in **Dual Diagnosis in Substance Abuse,** edited by Mark S. Gold and Andrew E. Slaby, 105-115. New York, NY: Marcel Dekker, 1991.

1.142. Clarke, J. Christopher and Wayne Wardman. "Agoraphobia Is a Form of Depression." in **Agoraphobia: A Clinical and Personal Account,** by J. Christopher Clarke and Wayne Wardman, 50-52. Sydney, NSW: Pergamon, 1985.

There appears to be a very close correlation between depression and agoraphobia. It is common to note that after agoraphobia has been successfully treated, the accompanying depression has lifted.

1.143. Clarke, J. Christopher and Wayne Wardman. "Depression." in **Agoraphobia: A Clinical and Personal Account,** by J. Christopher Clarke and Wayne Wardman, 37-38. Sydney, NSW: Pergamon, 1985.

Depression arises in agoraphobics because their agoraphobia prohibits them from doing ordinary everyday things. This makes agoraphobics feel helpless and frustrated. They cannot, for example, go for a walk or play golf.

1.144. Coccaro, Emil F. "Psychodynamic Aspects of Mood Disorders." Chapter in **Foundations of Psychiatry,** edited by Kenneth Davis, Howard Klar and Joseph T. Coyle, 263-269. Philadelphia, PA: W.B. Saunders, 1991.

1.145. Coleman, James C. "Guilt and Depression." in **Personality Dynamics and Effective Behavior,** by James C. Coleman, 335-336. Chicago, IL: Scott, Foresman and Company, 1960.

1.146. Colten, Mary Ellen, Susan Gore and Robert H. Aseltine, Jr. "Depression." in **Adolescent Stress: Causes and Consequences,** edited by Mary Ellen Colten and Susan Gore, 162. New York, NY: Aldine de Gruyter, 1991.

The Center for Epidemiologic Studies Depression Scale (CES-D) is the measure of depressive symptoms. This scale is a twenty-item self-report measure, which takes into account a week of depressive mood and feelings. Symptoms are clinically significant if the score is sixteen or higher.

1.147. Colten, Mary Ellen, Susan Gore and Robert H. Aseltine, Jr. "Depression and Other Problems." in **Adolescent Stress: Causes and Consequences,** edited by Mary Ellen Colten and Susan Gore, 170-171. New York, NY: Aldine de Gruyter, 1991.

1.148. Coon, Dennis. "Affective Psychosis: Peaks and Valleys." in **Introduction to Psychology: Exploration and Application,** Third Edition, by Dennis Coon, 485-487. St. Paul, MN: West Publishing, 1983.

1.149. Coon, Dennis. "Depression." in **Introduction to Psychology: Exploration and Application,** Third Edition, by Dennis Coon, 306. St. Paul, MN: West Publishing, 1983.

1.150. Coyne, James C. "Thinking Postcognitively about Depression." Chapter in **Comprehensive Handbook of Cognitive Therapy,** edited by Arthur Freeman, Karen M. Simon, Larry E. Beutler and Hal Arkowitz, 227-244. New York, NY: Plenum, 1989.

1.151. Craddock, Denis. "Depression." in **A Short Textbook of General Practice,** Third Edition, by Denis Craddock, 371. London: H.K. Lewis and Co., 1976.

Depression can be associated with diabetes or myxoedema, and with certain drugs, including methyl dopa, reserpine, and fenflunamine.

1.152. Craddock, Denis. "The Depressive Personality." in **A Short Textbook of General Practice**, Third Edition, by Denis Craddock, 84. London: H.K. Lewis and Co., 1976.

1.153. Craddock, Denis. "Endogenous Depression." in **A Short Textbook of General Practice**, Third Edition, by Denis Craddock, 372-374. London: H.K. Lewis and Co., 1976.

1.154. Craddock, Denis. "Post-Hysterectomy Depression." in **A Short Textbook of General Practice**, Third Edition, by Denis Craddock, 682. London: H.K. Lewis and Co., 1976.

1.155. Craddock, Denis. "Puerperal Depression." in **A Short Textbook of General Practice**, Third Edition, by Denis Craddock, 192-193. London: H.K. Lewis and Co., 1976.

1.156. Crowcroft, Andrew. "Feelings of Loss: Mourning and Depression." in **The Psychotic: Understanding Madness**, by Andrew Crowcroft, 93-108. Harmondsworth: Penguin, 1967.

A psychoanalytic approach - with reference to infancy, childhood, and depression in adulthood - elaborates on mourning and depression.

1.157. Custer, Robert and Harry Milt. "Anxiety, Depression, Omnipotence." in **When Luck Runs Out: Help for Compulsive Gamblers and Their Families**, by Robert Custer and Harry Milt, 86-89. New York, NY: Warner Books, 1985.

A tendency to be depressed and anxious is characteristic, during the youth and early adult life, of compulsive gamblers. Gambling is, in a way, an antidepressant for these persons. Gambling alters their mood, lifts them out of their depression.

1.158. Darley, John M., Sam Glucksberg, Leon J. Kamin and Ronald A. Kinchla. "Depression." in **Psychology**, by John M. Darley, Sam Glucksberg, Leon J. Kamin and Ronald A. Kinchla, 470-473. Englewood Cliffs, NJ: Prentice-Hall, 1981.

1.159. Davitz, Joel R. "Depression." in **The Language of Emotion**, by Joel R. Davitz, 45-47. New York, NY: Academic Press, 1969.

Depression is derived from "deprimere," a Latin word which means "to press down."

1.160. Dennis, Lorraine Bradt. "Depression." in **Psychology of Human Behavior for Nurses**, Third Edition, by Lorraine Bradt Dennis, 212-215. Philadelphia, PA: W.B. Saunders, 1967.

Severe and long-lasting depression has been associated with the concept of a nervous breakdown. This type of depression involves an unconscious self-punishing mechanism. The severely depressed person appears to have been a very conscientious child, who repressed guilt and feelings of worthlessness. Repression disappears when the person learns to divert elsewhere, other than to repress, societally unacceptable emotions. 1 cartoon illustration.

1.161. "Depression." in **The American Medical Association Family Medical Guide**, Revised and Updated, edited by Jeffrey R.M. Kunz and Asher J. Finkel, 106. New York, NY: Random House, 1987.

A series of questions, presented in schematic form, can be used to diagnose depression.

1.162. "Depression." in **The American Medical Association Family Medical Guide**, Revised and Updated, edited by Jeffrey R.M. Kunz and Asher J. Finkel, 301-302. New York, NY: Random House, 1987.

Symptoms, risks, options, treatment, and long-term prospects have to be considered in the management of depression.

1.163. Diamond, John. "Grief." in **Life Energy: Understanding and Transforming Your Emotions to Acheive Total Health**, by John Diamond, 172. New York, NY: Dodd, Mead and Company, 1985.

1.164. Diamond, John. "Melancholy." in **Life Energy: Understanding and Transforming Your Emotions to Achieve Total Health**, by John Diamond, 171-172. New York, NY: Dodd, Mead and Company, 1985.

1.165. Dorcus, Roy M. and G. Wilson Shaffer. "Manic-Depressive Psychoses." in **Textbook of Abnormal Psychology,** Third Edition, by Roy M. Dorcus and G. Wilson Shaffer, 337-341. Baltimore, MD: Williams and Wilkins, 1945.

Females constitute approximately 60% to 70% of manic-depressive psychotics. These individuals are usually short, stocky, and have thick necks. Extroverts become manic-depressives; introverts tend to become schizophrenics. Although ovarian and thyroid disorders are not uncommon in manic-depressives, no direct causal relationship appears to exist. 2 figures.

1.166. Dorcus, Roy M. and G. Wilson Shaffer. "Manic States." in **Textbook of Abnormal Psychology,** Third Edition, by Roy M. Dorcus and G. Wilson Shaffer, 341-343. Baltimore, MD: Williams and Wilkins, 1945.

1.167. Dorsey, John Morris. "Depression and Elation: The Meaning of Guilt." in **The Foundations of Human Nature: The Study of the Person,** by John Morris Dorsey, 236-239. New York, NY: Longmans, Green and Co., 1935.

1.168. Dowling, Colette. "Is Your Child Depressed?" Appendix in **You Mean I Don't Have to Feel This Way?: New Help for Depression, Anxiety, and Addiction,** by Colette Dowling, 235-237. New York, NY: Charles Scribner's Sons, 1991.

In a twenty-five item questionnaire on depression, the questionnaire respondant is asked, for each question, to check "never," "sometimes," or "always."

1.169. Epstein, Leon J. "Depression." in **Clinical Aspects of Aging,** Second Edition, edited by William Reichel, 132-133. Baltimore, MD: Williams and Wilkins, 1983.

Insomnia, weight loss, apathy, and hostility are some of the symptoms frequently found in most depressed elderly patients. Drug use or misuse can cause depression in these persons, as can various organic illnesses. Liver dysfunction and anemia are two of these illnesses.

1.170. Epstein, Leon J. "Mania." in **Clinical Aspects of Aging,** Second Edition, edited by William Reichel, 133-134. Baltimore, MD: Williams and Wilkins, 1983.

Mania in the elderly can be characterized, in part, by hyperactivity, decreased need for sleep, and heightened self-esteem.

Manic episodes may last from days to months. Lithium is the preferred treatment.

1.171. Ferster, C.B., Stuart Culbertson and Mary Carol Perrott Boren. "Clinical Depression." Chapter in **Behavior Principles,** Second Edition, by C.B. Ferster, Stuart Culbertson and Mary Carol Perrott Boren, 642-665. Englewood Cliffs, NJ: Prentice-Hall, 1975.

1.172. Fine, Reuben. "Depression." in **A History of Psychoanalysis,** by Reuben Fine, 407-408. New York, NY: Columbia University Press, 1979.

1.173. Fine, Reuben. "Mourning and Melancholia." in **The Development of Freud's Thought: From the Beginnings (1886-1900) through Id Psychology (1900-1914) to Ego Psychology (1914-1939),** by Reuben Fine, 210-214. New York, NY: Jason Aronson, 1973.

Freud viewed melancholia as a symptom, not as a separate illness, and allowed for the possibility an organic factor could explain some aspects of melancholia. He, nevertheless, believed melancholia could be adequately explained in psychological terms.

1.174. Fisher, S. "Pessimism in Depressed Individuals." in **Stress and the Perception of Control,** by S. Fisher, 228-235. London: Lawrence Erlbaum Associates, 1984.

1.175. Forrest, Gary G. "Alcoholism, Depression and Oral Rage." Chapter in **Alcoholism, Narcissism and Psychopathology,** by Gary G. Forrest, 98-120. Springfield, IL: Charles C. Thomas, 1983.

1.176. Frankl, Viktor E. "On the Psychology of Melancholia." in **The Doctor and the Soul: From Psychotherapy to Logotherapy,** Second Expanded Edition, by Viktor E. Frankl, translated by Richard and Clara Winston, 200-206. New York, NY: Vintage Books, 1973. Originally published as **Ärztliche Seelsorge,** Franz Deuticke, 1952.

1.177. Freudenberger, Herbert J. and Gail North. "Is It Burnout or Depression?" in **Women's Burnout: How to Spot It, How to Reverse It, and How to Prevent It,** by Herbert J. Freudenberger and Gail North, 19-21. Garden City, NY: Doubleday and Company, 1985. Reprint. Harmondsworth, Penguin, 1986.

Excessive stress and fatigue cause burnout, while loss causes depression. An erosion of energy and attitudes characterizes burnout, but sadness and a feeling of mourning characterize depression. The person burning out may be disenchanted at work, but not, perhaps, at home. The depressed person experiences little or no joy, regardless of the context - work or home. The depressed person feels defeated; the burned out person may use alcohol or drugs to fight the burnout.

1.178. Friedman, William. "The Experience of Time in Depression." in **About Time: Inventing the Fourth Dimension,** by William Friedman, 118-120. Cambridge, MA: MIT Press, 1990.

1.179. Fromm, Erich. "Chronic Depression-Boredom." in **The Anatomy of Human Destructiveness,** by Erich Fromm, 242-251. New York, NY: Holt, Rinehart and Winston, 1973.

1.180. Fromme, Allan. "Depression." in **Our Troubled Selves: A New and Positive Approach,** by Allan Fromme, 127-146. New York, NY: Farrar, Straus and Giroux, 1967.

1.181. Garre, Walter J. "Depression and Grief, Repressed Fury." Chapter in **The Missing Link: The Transition from Animal Instinct to the Human Mind, The Origin of the Human Mind,** by Walter J. Garre, 151-158. New York, NY: Philosophical Library, 1982.

Depression is a relatively new term which has replaced the word "melancholia," melancholia dating back to pre-Biblical times, King Saul having suffered from this illness. Hippocrates attributed melancholia to black bile. Aretaeus, a Roman physician, attempted to account for melancholia in terms of anger, grief, and other factors.

1.182. Gaylord, Susan A. and William W.K. Zung. "Affective Disorders among the Aging." Chapter in **Handbook of Clinical Gerontology,** Pergamon General Psychology Series 146, by Laura L. Carstensen and Barry A. Edelstein, 76-95. New York, NY: Pergamon, 1987.

1.183. Gelder, M.G. "Affective Disorders." in **Oxford Textbook of Medicine,** Second Edition, Volume 2, edited by D.J. Weatherall, J.G.G. Ledingham and D.A. Warrell, 25.8-25.10. Oxford: Oxford University Press, 1987.

The person afflicted with a depressive disorder will awaken early and have difficulty falling asleep after this. The person afflicted with an anxiety neurosis will have difficulty initially falling asleep, but will not generally experience early morning awakening. Mood will deteriorate in the morning in the depressed person. Mood will deteriorate later in the day in the anxious person. 2 tables. 4 references.

1.184. Gelder, Michael, Dennis Gath and Richard Mayou. "Affective Disorders." Chapter in **Oxford Textbook of Psychiatry,** Second Edition, by Michael Gelder, Dennis Gath and Richard Mayou, 217-267. Oxford: Oxford University Press, 1989.

1.185. Gelder, Michael, Dennis Gath and Richard Mayou. "The Classification of Minor Depressive Disorders." in **Oxford Textbook of Psychiatry,** Second Edition, by Michael Gelder, Dennis Gath and Richard Mayou, 158-159. Oxford: Oxford University Press, 1989.

1.186. Gelder, Michael, Dennis Gath and Richard Mayou. "Depressive Disorder." in **Oxford Textbook of Psychiatry,** Second Edition, by Michael Gelder, Dennis Gath and Richard Mayou, 868-869. Oxford: Oxford University Press, 1989.

A person, seriously depressed, may kill their spouse or children, and then commit suicide. A mother who has post-natal depression may kill her newborn child or her older children. Individuals who carry out these acts believe they do the victims a "favor" by sparing them the misery of living in a terrible world. Depressed persons, due to feelings of guilt and worthlessness, sometimes confess to crimes they did not commit.

1.187. Gelder, Michael, Dennis Gath and Richard Mayou. "Depressive Disorders." in **Oxford Textbook of Psychiatry,** Second Edition, by Michael Gelder, Dennis Gath and Richard Mayou, 787. Oxford: Oxford University Press, 1989.

1.188. Gelder, Michael, Dennis Gath and Richard Mayou. "Manic and Depressive Disorder." in **Oxford Textbook of Psychiatry,** Second Edition, by Michael Gelder, Dennis Gath and Richard Mayou, 820. Oxford: Oxford University Press, 1989.

The incidence of manic-depressive disorder, although rare before puberty, increases during adolescence. Depressive disorder, sleep disturbances, delusions, and hallucinations occur less frequently in adolescents than in adults suffering from depressive disorders. Lithium is usually effective in management of affective disorders which recur.

1.189. Gleitman, Henry. "Helplessness and Depression." in **Psychology,** by Henry Gleitman, 148-149. New York, NY: W.W. Norton and Company, 1981.

Martin Seligman believes depression in humans may be explicable in the way in which learned helplessness is accounted for in animals.

1.190. Gold, Mark S. "Depression." in **The Good News about Drugs and Alcohol: Curing, Treating and Preventing Substance Abuse in the New Age of Biopsychiatry,** by Mark S. Gold, 104-105. New York, NY: Villard Books, 1991.

There may be in the U.S. as many as 6 million alcoholics experiencing depression. Some symptoms are common to both alcoholism and depression. Insomnia and loss of energy are two examples. Liver or pancreas diseases and malnutrition can produce symptoms which mimic depression. A specific vitamin deficiency may contribute to a person's depression.

1.191. Goleman, Daniel and Jonathan Freedman. "The Causes of Depression." in **What Psychology Knows that Everyone Should,** by Daniel Goleman and Jonathan Freedman, 228-229. Lexington, MA: Lewis Publishing, 1981.

The causes of depression have been attributed to brain chemistry, genetics, and learned helplessness.

1.192. Goleman, Daniel and Jonathan Freedman. "Some Sad Facts about Depression." in **What Psychology Knows that Everyone Should,** by Daniel Goleman and Jonathan Freedman, 227-228. Lexington, MA: Lewis Publishing, 1981.

Statistics indicate that for every two depressed men, there are three depressed women. At any given time, one in eight Americans is severely depressed. These individuals cannot be simply cheered up.

1.193. Goleman, Daniel and Jonathan Freedman. "The Wild, Wild World of Manic-Depressives." in **What Psychology Knows that Everyone Should,** by Daniel Goleman and Jonathan Freedman, 229-230. Lexington, MA: Lewis Publishing, 1981.

Extreme talkativeness, distractability, and impulsive acts, lasting at least one week, are some of the major indicators a person is experiencing a manic episode.

1.194. Gomberg, Edith S. Lisansky. "Learned Helplessness, Depression, and Alcohol Problems of Women." Chapter in **Women in Crisis**, edited by Penelope Russianoff, 38-43. New York, NY: Human Sciences Press, 1981.

1.195. Goodwin, Donald W. "Alcoholism and Affective Disorders: The Basic Questions." Chapter in **Alcoholism and Clinical Psychiatry**, edited by Joel Solomon, 87-95. New York, NY: Plenum, 1982.

Manic-depressives and alcoholics kill themselves more often than any other group, alcoholism having been referred to as slow suicide. When alcoholics stop drinking, their depression often lifts. Female alcoholics, unlike male alcoholics, are more often depressed preceding heavy drinking. 39 references.

1.196. Gottlieb, Gary L. "Mental Status Examination: Assessing Cognitive Function and Depression." in **Review of General Psychiatry**, Third Edition, edited by Howard H. Goldman, 448-449. Norwalk, CT: Appleton and Lange, 1992.

The Mini-Mental State Examination (MMSE) is widely used to determine if additional evaluation is required to assess cognitive function.

1.197. Graham, John R. "Scale 2 (Depression)." in **MMPI-2: Assessing Personality and Psychopathology**, by John R. Graham, 55-58. New York, NY: Oxford University Press, 1990.

Dr. Graham is an authority on the Minnesota Multiphasic Personality Inventory (MMPI). The author of **The MMPI: A Practical Guide**, Dr. Graham uses this test regularly. He is one of the individuals responsible for revising the MMPI.

1.198. Gray, J. Stanley. "Depression." in **Psychology Applied to Human Affairs**, by J. Stanley Gray, 242. New York, NY: McGraw-Hill, 1954.

1.199. Green, Stephen A. "The Depression Response." in **Human Behavior: An Introduction for Medical Students**, edited by Alan Stoudemire, 333. Philadelphia, PA: J.B. Lippincott Company, 1990.

A depressed person will exhibit various behavioral changes. This person may quit a satisfying job or end a long-term marriage. This is in addition to complaints of, for example, fatigue or decreased libido. A depressed individual may be unwilling to provide a medical history.

1.200. Greenwood, James W., III and James W. Greenwood, Jr. "Depression." in **Managing Executive Stress: A Systems Approach,** by James W. Greenwood, III and James W. Greenwood, Jr., 121-122. New York, NY: John Wiley and Sons, 1979.

1.201. Groth-Marnat, Gary. "The Beck Depression Inventory." in **Handbook of Psychological Assessment,** Second Edition, by Gary Groth-Marnat, 102-103. New York, NY: John Wiley and Sons, 1990.

The Beck Depression Inventory (BDI), used to assess depression in psychiatric patients and normals, was first introduced in 1961. The 1971 revision correlated highly with the original version. There have been since 1961 over 1,000 research studies associated with the BDI. A person with a fifth-grade reading level can comprehend the twenty-one items. The self-administered inventory can be completed in five to ten minutes.

1.202. Grunberger, Bela. "A Study of Depression." Chapter in **Narcissism: Psychoanalytic Essays,** translated by Joyce S. Diamanti, 219-240. New York, NY: International Universities Press, 1979. Originally published as **Le Narcissisme: Essais de Psychanalyse,** Éditions Payot, 1971.

1.203. Hafen, Brent Q. and Kathryn J. Frandsen. "Depression." in **Youth Suicide: Depression and Loneliness,** by Brent Q. Hafen and Kathryn J. Frandsen, 27-28. Evergreen, CO: Cordillera Press, 1986.

The probability a depressed person will commit suicide increases as that person's depression decreases. A severely depressed person does not have sufficient motivation and energy to commit suicide. Although depression is a major cause of suicide, not every person who commits suicide is depressed. Some people commit suicide impulsively.

1.204. Hafen, Brent Q. and Kathryn J. Frandsen. "Depression." in **Youth Suicide: Depression and Loneliness,** by Brent Q. Hafen and Kathryn J. Frandsen, 93-97. Evergreen, CO: Cordillera Press, 1986.

Low self-esteem is both one of the most significant determinants and most significant indicators of depression. Teenagers least likely to experience depression have a strong attachment to parents and a strong relationship with peers. Depression can result from either a laissez-faire or authoritarian parental attitude toward child rearing. Depression is much less likely to result in a home environment in which teenagers can make a gradual transition into adulthood. Depressed parents tend to raise depressed children.

1.205. Hafen, Brent Q. and Kathryn J. Frandsen. "Depression." in **Youth Suicide: Depression and Loneliness**, by Brent Q. Hafen and Kathryn J. Frandsen, 147. Evergreen, CO: Cordillera Press, 1986.

A depressed adult may be sad, tearful, and feel hopeless. A depressed teenager may not only be like this, he or she may also be restless, defiant, or angry. The teenager will not necessarily fit the pattern of the depressed adult, especially if the teenager skips school or steals money.

1.206. Hafen, Brent Q. and Kathryn J. Frandsen. "Have You Been Feeling Depressed? For How Long?" in **Youth Suicide: Depression and Loneliness**, by Brent Q. Hafen and Kathryn J. Frandsen, 139-140. Evergreen, CO: Cordillera Press, 1986.

Any teenager, seriously depressed, is at considerable risk for suicide. The teenager, more depressed than the person who has had the blues for a few days or few weeks, is at high risk. The teenager who indicates he is coming out of a deep depression is at even greater risk.

1.207. Hafen, Brent Q. and Kathryn J. Frandsen. "He May Show One or More Signs of Serious Depression." in **Youth Suicide: Depression and Loneliness**, by Brent Q. Hafen and Kathryn J. Frandsen, 118-119. Evergreen, CO: Cordillera Press, 1986.

There are nineteen indicators a teenager may be seriously depressed. Sadness; low self-esteem; suicidal ideation; changes in appetite; and changes in weight are some of these indicators.

1.208. Hertel, Paula T. "Memory Impairment in Depressed and Anxious States." in **Memory Improvement: Implications for Memory Theory**, edited by Douglas J. Herrmann, Herbert Weingartner, Alan Searleman and Cathy McEvoy, 44-49. New York, NY: Springer-Verlag, 1992.

1.209. Hicks, Robert, Anna Okonek and John M. Davis. "Anxiety Versus Depression." in **Handbook on Stress and Anxiety,** by Irwin L. Kutash and Louis B. Schlesinger, 435. San Francisco, CA: Jossey-Bass, 1980.

1.210. Hilgard, Ernest R. and Richard C. Atkinson. "Cultural Determiners of Depression." in **Introduction to Psychology,** Fourth Edition, by Ernest R. Hilgard and Richard C. Atkinson, 534. New York, NY: Harcourt, Brace and World, 1967.

Depression in Sweden and Denmark results when people fail to achieve vitally important needs. Achievement is the need for Swedes; dependency is the need for Danes. Swedish parents encourage their children to be, for example, competetive and to gain early independence. Danish parents encourage their children to inhibit competition and to be dependent. Swedes become depressed to the point of suicide when they fail in their work. Danes become depressed when they lose a loved one with whom they had a dependent relationship. Norwegian children are discouraged from being like Swedish or Danish children in terms of ambition and dependence. Furthermore, Norwegian children have more freedom to express aggression. Swedes and Danes turn aggression inward. Norwegians turn aggression outward. Sweden and Denmark have among the world's highest suicide rates, Norway one of the lowest.

1.211. Hilgard, Ernest R. and Richard C. Atkinson. "Manic-Depressive Reactions." in **Introduction to Psychology,** Fourth Edition, by Ernest R. Hilgard and Richard C. Atkinson, 533-534. New York, NY: Harcourt, Brace and World, 1967.

The person who has hypermania may continually pace about, sing, shout obscenities, or scream. This person, confused and disoriented, may also hallucinate. Some hypermanic individuals may become physically violent or sexually aggressive. Sedatives and hydrotherapy may be required to reduce the hypermanic's intense excitement.

1.212. Hockberger, Robert S. "Depression and Suicide." Chapter in **The Clinical Practice of Emergency Medicine,** edited by Ann Harwood-Nuss, 1159-1161. Philadelphia, PA: J.B. Lippincott Company, 1991.

There are in the U.S. approximately 30,000 suicides annually. Seventy percent to 90% of suicide attempts are due to drug overdose. Markedly-depressed or at-risk suicidal patients should be kept in an area where there are no potentially dangerous objects. The SAD PERSONS score is used to assess potentially suicidal patients. 1 table. 39 references.

1.213. Hodges, William. "Genes and Depression." in **Psychology: Its Principles and Meanings**, by Lyle B. Bourne, Jr. and Bruce R. Ekstrand, 369. Hinsdale, IL: Dryden Press, 1973.

Research by F.J. Kallman and Ronald R. Fieve indicates an important relationship between heredity and depression.

1.214. Hodges, William. "Neurotic Depression." in **Psychology: Its Principles and Meanings**, by Lyle E. Bourne, Jr. and Bruce R. Ekstrand, 358-360. Hinsdale, IL: Dryden Press, 1973.

1.215. Horowitz, Leonard M., Rita de S. French and Craig A. Anderson. "Relation between Loneliness and Depression." in **Loneliness: A Sourcebook of Current Theory, Research and Therapy**, edited by Letitia Anne Peplau and Daniel Perlman, 189-191. New York, NY: John Wiley and Sons, 1982.

It was determined, with the aid of forty subjects, that a lonely person has certain characteristics of depression. However, a depressed person is not necessarily also a lonely person.

1.216. Hyman, Jane Wegscheider. "Mood and Behavior." Chapter in **The Light Book: How Natural and Artificial Light Affect Our Health, Mood, and Behavior**, by Jane Wegscheider Hyman, 87-113. Los Angeles, CA: Jeremy P. Tarcher, 1990.

1.217. Hyman, Steven and George W. Arana. "Suicide and Affective Disorders." Chapter in **Suicide: Understanding and Responding: Harvard Medical School Perspectives**, edited by Douglas Jacobs and Herbert N. Brown, 171-181. Madison, CT: International Universities Press, 1990.

1.218. Ilfeld, Frederic W., Jr. "Marital Stressors, Coping Styles, and Symptoms of Depression." Chapter in **Handbook of Stress: Theoretical and Clinical Aspects**, edited by Leo Goldberger and Shlomo Breznitz, 482-495. New York, NY: Free Press, 1982.

1.219. Imboden, John B. and Joseph T. Coyle. "Affective Disorders." Chapter in **The Principles and Practice of Medicine**, Twenty-First Edition, edited by A. McGehee Harvey, Richard J. Johns, Victor A. McKusick, Albert H. Owens, Jr. and Richard S. Ross, 1367-1372. Norwalk, CT: Appleton-Century-Crofts, 1984.

The person who, early in life, experienced traumatic loss and developed an increased need for approval from others is the person, who will likely react with depression to current losses. Losses may relate to a number of things, including job, physical health, and social standing. 1 table. 11 references.

1.220. Jaffe, Jerome H. and Domenic A. Ciraulo. "Alcoholism and Depression." Chapter in **Psychopathology and Addictive Disorders,** edited by Roger E. Meyer, 293-320. New York, NY: Guilford Press, 1986.

1.221. Jellinek, Michael S. and David B. Herzog. "Depression." in **Massachusetts General Hospital Handbook of General Hospital Psychiatry,** Third Edition, edited by Ned H. Cassem, 494. St. Louis, MO: Mosby Year Book, 1991.

1.222. Kagan, Jerome, Ernest Havemann and Julius Segal. "Origins of Mood Disorders." in **Psychology: An Introduction,** Fifth Edition, by Jerome Kagan, Ernest Havemann and Julius Segal, 442-443. San Diego, CA: Harcourt Brace Jovanovich, 1984.

There is evidence there is a genetic basis, and brain-chemistry-imbalance basis, for mood disorders. It has been found that blood relatives have similar problems three times as often as adopted relatives. Drugs effective against depression seem to increase in the brain the availability of the neurotransmitter noradrenalin.

1.223. Kagan, Jerome, Ernest Havemann and Julius Segal. "The Two Poles of Manic-Depressive Illness." in **Psychology: An Introduction,** Fifth Edition, by Jerome Kagan, Ernest Havemann and Julius Segal, 441-442. San Diego, CA: Harcourt Brace Jovanovich, 1984.

No task seems insurmountable to manic persons. They may feel they can discover a cure for cancer, end racial prejudice, or do both these things - and others. The thoughts of manic persons can change rapidly and without any apparent logic.

1.224. Kaplan, Harold I. and Benjamin J. Sadock. "Mood (Affective) Disorders." in **Pocket Handbook of Clinical Psychiatry,** by Harold I. Kaplan and Benjamin J. Sadock, 81-95. Baltimore, MD: Williams and Wilkins, 1990.

1.225. Kendler, Howard H. "Depressive Reactions." in **Basic Psychology,** Third Edition, by Howard H. Kendler, 598. Menlo

Park, CA: W.A. Benjamin, 1974.

Neurotic depression is similar to learned helplessness and to despair reactions experienced by infant monkeys separated from their mothers.

1.226. Kendler, Howard H. "The Etiology of Manic-Depressive Psychosis." in **Basic Psychology,** Third Edition, by Howard H. Kendler, 611-612. Menlo Park, CA: W.A. Benjamin, 1974.

Body build has been associated with manic-depressive psychosis, stocky builds, that is, mesomorphic endomorphs, tending to predominate among manic-depressive persons.

1.227. Kendler, Howard H. "Involutional Melancholia." in **Basic Psychology,** Third Edition, by Howard H. Kendler, 612-613. Menlo Park, CA: W.A. Benjamin, 1974.

Involutional melancholia usually occurs in women several years after menopause, and in men between sixty-one and sixty-five years of age. Persons most likely to be afflicted have obsessive-compulsive personalities.

1.228. Kendler, Howard H. "Psychotic Depressive Reaction." in **Basic Psychology,** Third Edition, by Howard H. Kendler, 613. Menlo Park, CA: W.A. Benjamin, 1974.

There is no history of depressions/mood swings in persons who experience psychotic depressive reaction, and no marked genetic involvement.

1.229. Kennedy, Eugene. "The Core of Depression." Chapter in **On Becoming a Counsellor: A Basic Guide for Non-Professional Counsellors,** by Eugene Kennedy, 166-171. New York, NY: Continuum, 1977.

Although suicidal persons, directly or indirectly, tell other persons about their suicidal plans, other persons do not always accurately perceive what is communicated. This was exemplified in the on-air suicide of a Florida, television talk-show host. The host, a twenty-nine-year-old woman, who, according to her mother, did not have close friends, told co-workers about her suicidal intentions. Co-workers did not believe she was serious. The host had been depressed. 12 references.

1.230. Kennedy, Eugene. "Depression." Chapter in **Crisis Counseling: An Essential Guide for Nonprofessional Counselors,**

by Eugene Kennedy, 35-42. New York, NY: Continuum, 1984.

1.231. Kennedy, Eugene. "The Everyman Illness: Depression." Chapter in **On Becoming a Counselor: A Basic Guide for Non-Professional Counselors,** by Eugene Kennedy, 152-158. New York, NY: Continuum, 1977.

1.232. Kennedy, Eugene. "What Depresses People." Chapter in **On Becoming a Counselor: A Basic Guide for Non-Professional Counselors,** by Eugene Kennedy, 159-165. New York, NY: Continuum, 1977.

1.233. Khan, Aman U. "Depression." in **Psychiatric Emergencies in Pediatrics,** by Aman U. Khan, 97-105. Chicago, IL: Year Book Medical, 1979.

1.234. Kimmel, Douglas C. "Depression." in **Adulthood and Aging: An Interdisciplinary Developmental View,** Third Edition, by Douglas C. Kimmel, 545-546. New York, NY: John Wiley and Sons, 1990.

1.235. Kirkpatrick, Jean. "Understanding Your Depression." Chapter in **Goodbye Hangovers, Hello Life: Self-Help for Women,** by Jean Kirkpatrick, 43-55. New York, NY: Atheneum, 1986.

1.236. Klarreich, Samuel H. "The Depressive Type A." in **The Stress Solution: A Rational Approach to Increasing Corporate and Personal Effectiveness,** by Samuel H. Klarreich, 95-96. Toronto, ON: Key Porter Books, 1988.

Answering "yes" or "no" to ten questions may help determine if a person may be a candidate for burnout.

1.237. Klein, Melanie. "A Note on Depression in the Schizophrenic." Chapter in **Envy and Gratitude and Other Works 1946-1963,** by Melanie Klein, 264-267. London: Hogarth Press, 1975.

1.238. Knopf, Irwin J. "Depressive Reaction." in **Childhood Psychopathology: A Developmental Approach,** by Irwin J. Knopf, 339. Englewood Cliffs, NJ: Prentice-Hall, 1979.

1.239. Kraft, William F. "Depression." in **A Psychology of Nothingness**, by William F. Kraft, 38-45. Philadelphia, PA: Westminster Press, 1974.

Loss is a major factor in depression. A depressed person has lost someone or something and part of themselves. A depressed person who looks deeper into their own life and realizes nothing makes sense anymore experiences existential depression. This person looks inward and outward to regain meaning.

1.240. Kruglanski, Arie W. "Are Depressives Wiser?" in **Lay Epistemics and Human Knowledge: Cognitive and Motivational Bases**, by Arie W. Kruglanski, 213-215. New York, NY: Plenum, 1989.

1.241. LaFrance, Marianne and Clara Mayo. "Depression." in **Moving Bodies: Nonverbal Communication in Social Relationships**, by Marianne LaFrance and Clara Mayo, 53. Monterey, CA: Brooks/Cole, 1978.

Severely depressed people have downcast eyes - the averted gaze, have little eye contact with other people, and droop their head and mouth. Electronic analysis has demonstrated significant reduction in pitch and loudness, regarding normal range of variation. Tempo is reduced and there is no resonance.

1.242. Lampl-De Groot, Jeanne. "Depression and Aggression: A Contribution to the Theory of the Instinctual Drives." Chapter in **The Development of the Mind: Psychoanalytic Papers on Clinical and Theoretical Problems**, by Jeanne Lampl-De Groot, 213-230. N.p., International Universities Press, 1965.

1.243. Lazarus, Richard S. "Neurotic Depression." in **Adjustment and Personality**, by Richard S. Lazarus, 346-347. New York, NY: McGraw-Hill, 1961.

A precipitating event usually brings about neurotic (reactive) depression. Neurotic depressives have unconscious feelings of hostility. These persons react with guilt and excessive depression to a personal loss.

1.244. Lehner, George F.J. and Ella Kube. "Depressive Reactions." in **The Dynamics of Personal Adjustment**, Second Edition, by George F.J. Lehner and Ella Kube, 152-153. Englewood Cliffs, NJ: Prentice-Hall, 1964.

A person may try to deal with anxiety by experiencing a depressive reaction. Dejection is a moderate form of depression. A neurotic depressive reaction is characterized by symptoms in acute form. Reactive depression is synonymous with neurotic depressive reaction. Loss of initiative, feelings of worthlessness, and guilt are examples of symptoms associated with depression.

1.245. Lehner, George F.J. and Ella Kube. "Involutional Melancholia." in **The Dynamics of Personal Adjustment,** Second Edition, by George F.J. Lehner and Ella Kube, 171-172. Englewood Cliffs, NJ: Prentice-Hall, 1964.

Involutional melancholia occurs in women who are between approximately forty and fifty-five years of age and in men who are approximately between fifty and sixty-five. There is a combination of depression and restlessness in this illness, which has been attributed to change-of-life physiological and endocrine changes. The past cannot be relived and the future offers a decreasing number of opportunities for persons with this condition.

1.246. Lehner, George F.J. and Ella Kube. "The Manic-Depressive Psychosis." in **The Dynamics of Personal Adjustment,** Second Edition, by George F.J. Lehner and Ella Kube, 169-171. Englewood Cliffs, NJ: Prentice-Hall, 1964.

Manic-depressive psychosis consists of a manic phase and a depressive phase. There is, in some individuals, only the manic phase, in other persons only the depressive phase, and in other individuals a combination of manic and depressive phases. Rapid heart action, high blood pressure, and insomnia are three characteristics of the manic phase. Indifference to other people, constipation, and guilt are a few characteristics of the depressive phase. Menstruation may stop in the female manic-depressive when she is in the depressive phase.

1.247. Lever, Judy and Michael G. Brush. "Depression." in **Premenstrual Tension,** by Judy Lever and Michael G. Brush, 28-30. New York, NY: McGraw-Hill, 1981.

1.248. Lewin, Bertram D. "Literary Survey of Depression and Elation." Chapter in **The Psychoanalysis of Elation,** by Bertram D. Lewin, 20-51. New York, NY: W.W. Norton and Company, 1950.

1.249. Light, William J. Haugen, "Depression, Dependency, Denial and Dysphoria." in **Psychodynamics of Alcoholism: A**

Current Synthesis, by William J. Haugen Light, 137-175. Springfield, IL: Charles C. Thomas, 1986.

1.250. Lindenmayer, Jean-Pierre. "The Depressed Patient." in **Principles and Practice of Emergency Medicine**, Volume 2, Third Edition, edited by George R. Schwartz, C. Gene Cayten, Mary Anne Mangelsen, Thom A. Mayer and Barbara K. Hanke, 2662-2666. Philadelphia, PA: Lea and Febiger, 1992.

There are various things to keep in mind when evaluating patient suicide potential. For example, men commit suicide more often than do women. Divorced and widowed persons have a higher suicide rate than do married persons. A detailed plan on how the suicide will be carried out is a third thing to note. A depressed person, who suddenly appears to feel better, may have made the final decision to commit suicide. The patient who, in the past, has attempted suicide is at higher risk of suicide than the patient with no previous history of attempted suicide. 2 tables. 6 references.

1.251. Lowen, Alexander. "Depression and Illusion." in **Pleasure: A Creative Approach to Life**, by Alexander Lowen, 199-206. New York, NY: Coward-McCann, 1970.

1.252. MacLean, George. "Depressive Disorders in Children and Adolescents." Chapter in **Suicide in Children and Adolescents**, edited by George MacLean, 41-64. Toronto, ON: Hogrefe and Huber, 1990.

1.253. Macleod, John. "Depressive Psychoneurosis." in **Davidson's Principles and Practice of Medicine: A Textbook for Students and Doctors**, Fourteenth Edition, edited by John Macleod, 690. Edinburgh: Churchill Livingstone, 1984.

Depressive psychoneurosis often manifests itself after a patient loses an important person through, for example, death or divorce. This loss reflects a loss which occurred when the patient was younger.

1.254. Mahrer, Alvin R. "Depression." in **Experiencing: A Humanistic Theory of Psychology and Psychiatry**, by Alvin R. Mahrer, 85-86. New York, NY: Brunner/Mazel, 1978.

1.255. Malmquist, Carl P. "Depressions in Childhood and Adolescence." Chapter in **New Directions in Childhood Psychopathology, Volume 2: Deviations in Development**, edited by Saul I. Harrison and John F. McDermott, Jr., 831-856. New York, NY: International Universities Press, 1982.

1.256. Malmquist, Carl P. "Introduction: Depressions in Childhood and Adolescence." Chapter in **New Directions in Childhood Psychopathology, Volume 2: Deviations in Development,** edited by Saul I. Harrison and John F. McDermott, Jr., 827-830. New York, NY: International Universities Press, 1982.

Twenty thousand suicides are recorded annually in the U.S. Eighty percent of these suicides are attributed to depression.

1.257. "Manic-depression." in **The American Medical Association Family Medical Guide,** Revised and Updated, edited by Jeffrey R.M. Kunz and Asher J. Finkel, 302-303. New York, NY: Random House, 1987.

It is very rare for manic-depression to be caused by a severe infection, stroke, or brain injury. Rarer than depression, manic depression tends to occur in families.

1.258. Martin, Nicholas and Rosemary Jardine. "Delusions-Symptoms-States Inventory: Anxiety and Depression Scales (DSSI/sAD)." in **Hans Eysenck: Consensus and Controversy,** edited by Sohan Modgil and Celia Modgil, 16-17. Philadelphia, PA: Falmer, 1986.

1.259. Mayerson, Evelyn Wilde. "The Depressed Patient." in **Putting the Ill at Ease,** by Evelyn Wilde Mayerson, 164-165. Hagerstown, MD: Harper and Row, 1976.

A high-risk suicide is the physically-sick older male, who lives alone. He may worry, while in hospital, who will help care for him, after he is discharged. He may also worry about the effect of limited functioning on his life style. Suicide is most likely when he is coming out of or entering a deep depression. It is, at this time, that he has sufficient motivation and energy to kill himself.

1.260. Mayerson, Evelyn Wilde. "Depression." in **Putting the Ill at Ease,** by Evelyn Wilde Mayerson, 90-93. Hagerstown, MD: Harper and Row, 1976.

Asking depressed patients if they are contemplating suicide is a sensitive matter for many health professionals. Determining if the patients have a definite plan is even more unsettling for these caregivers. Depressed patients, however, do have suicidal ideas. Suicidal potential should be evaluated. Doing so will indicate to depressed patients that their physician, or other health professional, is seriously concerned about their condition.

1.261. McGee, Mark G. and David W. Wilson. "Causes." in **Psychology: Science and Application**, by Mark G. McGee and David W. Wilson, 403-404. St. Paul, MN: West Publishing, 1984.

Biological, psychoanalytic, behavioral, and cognitive models have been formulated to account for affective disorders.

1.262. McIntire, Roger W. "Teenage Depression." in **Losing Control of Your Teenager: Ten Rules for Raising an Adult while Keeping a Friend**, by Roger W. McIntire, 165-166. Amherst, MA: Human Resource Development Press, 1985.

1.263. McLellan, Tom, Alicia Bragg and John Cacciola. "Depression." in **Escape from Anxiety and Stress**, by Tom McLellan, Alicia Bragg and John Cacciola, 45-48. New York, NY: Chelsea House Publishers, 1986.

1.264. McMahon, Frank B. and Sarah B. Resnick. "Manic-Depressive Reactions." in **Behind the Mask: Our Psychological World**, by Frank B. McMahon and Sarah B. Resnick, 186-187. Englewood Cliffs, NJ: Prentice-Hall, 1973.

Neurotic depression is the most common type of depression. It is caused by a specific disappointment. Duration and severity differentiate psychotic from neurotic depression. Psychotic depression stems from deep psychological problems. The neurotic person, unlike the psychotic individual, does not completely lose touch with reality.

1.265. McNeil, Elton B. "Mania and Depression." in **The Psychology of Being Human**, by Elton B. McNeil, 475. San Francisco, CA: Canfield Press, 1974.

Manic-depressive disorders existed even during the time of Homer and Hippocrates. The first manic-depressive attack usually occurs when a person is between twenty and thirty years old. This condition occurs more frequently in women than in men. Females constitute approximately 70% of hospitalized manic-depressives.

1.266. Medley, E. Scott. "Depression." in **Common Health Problems in Medical Practice**, by E. Scott Medley, 313-314. Baltimore, MD: Williams and Wilkins, 1982.

Depression, very common in the elderly, accounts for almost one-third of all suicides. The deaths of children or grandchildren may lead to depression and suicide. Loneliness, accompanied by bitterness and frustration when an elderly person has been abandoned by family, may also contribute to suicide. Fear of being assaulted and robbed and fear of death may precipitate suicide. The tricyclic antidepressants - for example, imipramine (Tofranil), amitriptyline (Elavil), and doxepin (Sinequan) - are used to treat the depressed elderly. Drowsiness, dry mouth, and constipation are common side effects of these medications.

1.267. Menninger, Karl A. "Psychological Mechanisms of Melancholia." in **The Human Mind**, Third Edition, by Karl A. Menninger, 121. New York, NY: Alfred A. Knopf, 1955.

1.268. Menninger, Karl A. "Symptoms of Melancholia." in **The Human Mind**, Third Edition, by Karl A. Menninger, 120-121. New York, NY: Alfred A. Knopf, 1955.

1.269. Millenson, J.R. and Julian C. Leslie. "Depression." in **Principles of Behavioral Analysis**, Second Edition, by J.R. Millenson and Julian C. Leslie, 474-477. New York, NY: Macmillan, 1979.

Helplessness training is a behavioral paradigm in animals that, according to Maier, Seligman, and Solomon (1969), parallels features of depression. Activity-cycle disruption is another behavioral paradigm that parallels characteristics of depression. The latter paradigm is associated with Baltzer and Weis-Krantz (1975). 2 figures.

1.270. Miller, William R., Robert A. Rosellini and Martin E.P. Seligman. "Learned Helplessness and Depression." in **Psychopathology: Experimental Models**, edited by Jack D. Maser and Martin E.P. Seligman, 104-130. San Francisco, CA: W.H. Freeman and Company, 1977.

1.271. Mills, Ivor H. "Interaction between Arousal and Depression." in **Smoking Behaviour: Physiological and Psychological Influences**, edited by Raymond E. Thornton, 4-7. Edinburgh: Churchill Livingstone, 1978.

1.272. Mitchell, John J. "Adolescent Depression." in **The Adolescent Predicament**, by John J. Mitchell, 111-112. Toronto, ON: Holt, Rinehart and Winston of Canada, 1975.

1.273. "Mood Disorders." Chapter in **The Merck Manual of Diagnosis and Therapy**, Sixteenth Edition, 1592-1614. Rahway, NJ: Merck Research Laboratories, 1992.

Seven selected causes of depression: (1) pharmacological (amphetamine withdrawal); (2) infectious (tuberculosis); (3) endocrinological (Cushing's disease); (4) collagen-vascular (rheumatoid arthritis); (5) neurological (stroke); (6) nutritional (pellagra); and (7) neoplastic (cancer of the pancreas). 6 tables.

1.274. Morehouse, Ellen R. "Depression and Guilt." in **Youth and Alcohol Abuse: Readings and Resources**, edited by Carla Martindell Felsted, 137. Phoenix, AZ: Oryx, 1986.

1.275. Moretti, Marlene M., Lisa A. Feldman and Brian F. Shaw. "Depression." in **Handbook of the Brief Psychotherapies**, edited by Richard A. Wells and Vincent J. Giannetti, 222-224. New York, NY: Plenum, 1990.

Aaron Beck's explanation of how individuals view themselves, the world, and the future - the cognitive triad - helps understand depression. Depressed individuals have a strong negative bias regarding self-referent information processing. These individuals perceive themselves as, for example, inadequate and helpless. They, furthermore, view their interrelationships as rejection. Depressed persons also feel hopeless about the future. This, very concisely, is the cognitive model of depression.

1.276. Morgan, Clifford T., Richard A. King and Nancy M. Robinson. "Depressive Behavior." in **Introduction to Psychology**, Sixth Edition, by Clifford T. Morgan, Richard A. King and Nancy M. Robinson, 561. New York, NY: McGraw-Hill, 1979.

In the U.S., approximate number of people with depressive symptoms hospitalized annually: 125,000. Number treated annually as outpatients: about 200,000.

1.277. Morris, William N. "The Continuity Hypothesis." Chapter in **Mood: The Frame of Mind**, by William N. Morris, 159-197. New York, NY: Springer-Verlag, 1989.

1.278. Morse, Donald Roy and M. Lawrence Furst. "Depression." in **Stress for Success: A Holistic Approach to Stress and Its Management**, by David Roy Morse and M. Lawrence Furst, 105-106. New York, NY: Van Nostrand Reinhold, 1979.

According to psychiatrist Richard Sword, there is a depression-prone personality. Some of the characteristics of this personality: hard worker, ambitious, high sense of integrity, never gets mad, pleasant to everyone.

1.279. Mowbray, R.M. and T. Ferguson Rodger. "Depression." in **Psychology in Relation to Medicine**, Fourth Edition, by R.M. Mowbray and T. Ferguson Rodger, 332-333. Edinburgh: Churchill Livingstone, 1973.

1.280. Moyer, Ellen. "Does Depression Have Something to Do with RA?" in **Arthritis: Questions You Have...Answers You Need**, by Ellen Moyer, 153-154. Allentown, PA: People's Medical Society, 1993.

Dr. Esther Sternberg, National Institute of Mental Health (NIMH), believes that a stress-hormone deficiency may be associated with both rheumatoid arthritis (RA) and depression.

1.281. Mueller, L. Ann and Katherine Ketcham. "Depression." in **Recovering: How to Get and Stay Sober**, by L. Ann Mueller and Katherine Ketcham, 237-238. New York, NY: Bantam Books, 1987.

Between 50% and 90% of alcoholics being treated have symptoms of depression. Most alcoholics have endogenous depression - depression due to internal causes, for example, blood sugar abnormalities. Calcium deficiency and hypoglycemia can also cause depression.

1.282. Munroe, Ruth L. "Depressive States." in **Schools of Psychoanalytic Thought: An Exposition, Critique, and Attempt at Integration**, by Ruth L. Munroe, 288-290. New York, NY: Dryden Press, 1955.

1.283. Myers, Michael F. "Married Women Physicians and Depression." in **Doctors' Marriages: A Look at the Problems and Their Solutions**, by Michael F. Myers, 96-97. New York, NY: Plenum, 1988.

1.284. Nabarro, Elizabeth. "Depression." in **The Making of a Counsellor**, edited by Ellen Noonan and Laurence Spurling, 70-71. London: Routledge, 1992.

1.285. Norman, William H., Belinda A. Johnson and Ivan W. Miller, III. "Depression: A Behavioral-Cognitive Approach." in **Behavior Modification with Women**, edited by Elaine A. Blechman, 275-307. New York, NY: Guilford Press, 1984.

1.286. O'Kelly, Lawrence I. and Frederick A. Muckler. "Agitated Depression." in **Introduction to Psychopathology,** Second Edition, by Lawrence I. O'Kelly and Frederick A. Muckler, 313-314. Englewood Cliffs, NJ: Prentice-Hall, 1955.

1.287. Olsen, Ole Andkjaer and Simo Køppe. "Melancholia and Mania." in **Freud's Theory of Psychoanalysis**, by Ole Andkjaer Olsen and Simon Køppe, translated by Jean-Christian Delay and Carl Pedersen, 249-250. New York, NY: New York University Press, 1988.

1.288. Olson, Ken. "The Advantages of Being Depressed." in **Can You Wait Till Friday?: The Psychology of Hope,** by Ken Olson, 150-151. Greenwich, CT: Fawcett, 1975.

Some depressed people see a powerful advantage in being depressed. Example: depression can be used to control a relationship. Furthermore, many valid excuses can be attributed to depression. Good diet and exercise can help effectively fight depression.

1.289. Olson, Ken. "Depression as Anger Turned Inward." in **Can You Wait Till Friday?: The Psychology of Hope,** by Ken Olson, 140-143. Greenwich, CT: Fawcett, 1975.

Depression can result when anger is turned inward. Persistent headaches are an example of a physical symptom, representing an inability to express anger.

1.290. Olson, Ken. "Depression from Guilt." in **Can You Wait Till Friday?: The Psychology of Hope,** by Ken Olson, 143-147. Greenwich, CT: Fawcett, 1975.

Parents and religions induce guilt into children and others in order to control these persons. Children and others are then motivated by fear or respect for authority. Incorrect decisions or belefs about oneself also produce guilt and depression. One way to prevent depression due to guilt is not to accept guilt for virtually anything that occurs near oneself. Another is to try forgiving oneself.

1.291. Olson, Ken. "Fatigue-Debt Depression." in **Can You Wait Till Friday?: The Psychology of Hope**, by Ken Olson, 147. Greenwich, CT: Fawcett, 1975.

Fatigue-debt depression is associated with the person who works too hard and too long. This person is exhausted, yet experiences insomnia. This easily-irritated person must learn how to relax.

1.292. Olson, Ken. "Reactive Depression." in **Can You Wait Till Friday?: The Psychology of Hope**, by Ken Olson, 148-150. Greenwich, CT: Fawcett, 1975.

Job loss, Christmas, and divorce can be experiences associated with reactive depression, depression associated with a person's reaction to various life circumstances, in which there is a loss or the feeling that an experience was not as pleasurable or as fulfilling as it should have been.

1.293. Olson, Ken. "Self-Pity Depression." in **Can You Wait Till Friday?: The Psychology of Hope**, by Ken Olson, 139-140. Greenwich, CT: Fawcett, 1975.

The person who experiences self-pity depression makes it difficult for other persons - because of the self-pity - to be near this person. The person who experiences self-pity depression repels other people.

1.294. Olson, Ken. "Symptoms of Depression." in **Can You Wait Till Friday?: The Psychology of Hope**, by Ken Olson, 138-139. Greenwich, CT: Fawcett, 1975.

A feeling of hopelessness, life events occurring in slow motion, boredom, lack of motivation, insomnia, and reliance on alcohol are some of the characteristics of the depressed person.

1.295. Orme, J.E. "Depression and Mania." in **Time, Experience and Behaviour**, by J.E. Orme, 80-81. London: Iliffe Books, 1969.

1.296. Orr, Douglass W. and Nancy Orr Adams. "Depression." in **Life Cycle Counseling: Guidelines for Helping People**, by Douglass W. Orr and Nancy Orr Adams, 201-202. Springfield, IL: Charles C. Thomas, 1987.

Endocrine changes, fatigue, and the responsibilities of motherhood are the probable causes of postpartum depression. The mother, unconsciously, resents the baby. Consciously, she is depressed. 1 reference.

1.297. Ouslander, Joseph G., Dan Osterweil and John Morley. "Depression." in **Medical Care in the Nursing Home,** by Joseph G. Ouslander, Dan Osterweil and John Morley, 115-121. New York, NY: McGraw-Hill, 1991.

The Yesavage Geriatric Depression Scale (YGDS) consists of questions concerning how the respondant felt during the past week. The respondant chooses the best answer, responding with a "yes" or "no." There are thirty questions. Memory, crying, and social gatherings are a few topics covered by the questions. 4 tables. 1 figure.

1.298. Parkins, E.J. "Depression." Chapter in **Equilibration, Mind, and Brain: Toward an Integrated Psychology,** by E.J. Parkins, 135-142. New York, NY: Praeger, 1990.

Certain actions are characteristic of the depressed person. The depressed person will draw a negative conclusion without the aid of supporting data. The depressed person will focus on a particular detail and will often overlook more important information. This type of person will also overgeneralize. A fourth characteristic of the depressed person is dichotomous thinking. He or she will view someone or something in black-and-white, all-good or all-bad terms. He or she will, furthermore, frequently relate negative events to themselves, even though there is no real justification to do so.

1.299. Parkins, E.J. "Interrelationship between Schizophrenia, Depression, Epilepsy, and Parkinsonian Disorders," Chapter in **Equilibration, Mind, and Brain: Toward an Integrated Psychology,** by E.J. Parkins, 155-159. New York, NY: Praeger, 1990.

1.300. Patterson, C.H. "Depressions." in **Theories of Counseling and Psychotherapy,** by C.H. Patterson, 256. New York, NY: Harper and Row, 1973.

1.301. Patterson, C.H. "The Manic-Depressive Reactions." in **Theories of Counseling and Psychotherapy,** by C.H. Patterson, 256. New York, NY: Harper and Row, 1973.

There is, in the personality of the individual who experiences manic-depressive reactions, an equilibrium between repressed and repressing forces. An event can disturb this equilibrium, precipitating a reaction. A manic or depressive phase may result first.

1.302. Patterson, C.H. "Melancholia." in **Theories of Counseling and Psychotherapy,** by C.H. Patterson, 436. New York, NY: Harper and Row, 1973.

1.303. Pembrook, Linda. "Fatigue as Masked Depression." Chapter in **How to Beat Fatigue,** by Linda Pembrook, 197-214. New York, NY: Avon Books, 1975.

The main indicator of depression is fatigue. Low blood sugar levels, high temperatures, poorly-ventilated work areas, and emotional behaviors contribute to fatigue. 4 references.

1.304. Perrez, Meinrad and Michael Reicherts. "Depressed People Coping with Aversive Situations." Chapter in **Stress, Coping, and Health: A Situation-Behavior Approach Theory, Methods, Applications,** by Meinrad Perrez and Michael Reicherts, 103-111. Seattle, WA: Hogrefe and Huber, 1992.

1.305. Petersen, Anne C., Robert E. Kennedy and Patricia Sullivan. "Depression." in **Adolescent Stress: Causes and Consequences,** edited by Mary Ellen Colten and Susan Gore, 101-102. New York, NY: Aldine de Gruyter, 1991.

1.306. "Postpartum Depression." in **The American Medical Association Family Medi-al Guide,** Revised and Updated, edited by Jeffrey R.M. Kunz and Asher J. Finkel, 658. New York, NY: Random House, 1987.

The sudden change in body hormones, a sense of anticlimax, tiredness, apprehension, and under-confidence all probably contribute to postpartum depression. The support of family and friends can contribute to the mother overcoming this depression. If this does not work, an antidepressant drug, counseling or hospitalization should solve the problem.

1.307. Prugh, Dane G. "Psychoneurotic Disorders of the Depressive Type." in **The Psychosocial Aspects of Pediatrics**, by Dane G. Prugh, 289-291. Philadelphia, PA: Lea and Febiger, 1983.

1.308. Rabkin, Judith Godwin. "Stress and Depressive Disorders." in **Handbook of Stress: Theoretical and Clinical Aspects**, edited by Leo Goldberger and Shlomo Breznitz, 577-581. New York, NY: Free Press, 1982.

1.309. Rapaport, David. "Edward Bibring's Theory of Depression." Chapter in **The Collected Papers of David Rapaport**, edited by Merton M. Gill, 758-773. New York, NY: Basic Books, 1967.

David Rapaport's paper was presented at the Bibring Memorial Meeting, Boston Psychoanalytic Association, April 14, 1959. 13 references.

1.310. Rathus, Spencer A. and Jeffrey S. Nevid. "Depression." in **Psychology and the Challenges of Life: Adjustment and Growth**, Fourth Edition, by Spencer A. Rathus and Jeffrey S. Nevid, 210-211. New York, NY: Holt, Rinehart and Winston, 1989.

1.311. Rathus, Spencer A. and Jeffrey S. Nevid. "Major Depression." in **Psychology and the Challenges of Life: Adjustment and Growth**, Fourth Edition, by Spencer A. Rathus and Jeffrey S. Nevid, 290-291. New York, NY: Holt, Rinehart and Winston, 1989.

1.312. Rehm, Lynn P. "Assessment of Depression." Chapter in **Behavioral Assessment: A Practical Handbook**, Third Edition, Pergamon General Psychology Series 65, edited by Alan S. Bellack and Michel Hersen, 313-364. New York, NY: Pergamon, 1988.

There are a number of scales used to assess depression, including: (1) Beck Depression Inventory (BDI); (2) Center for Epidemiological Studies' Depression Scale (CES-D); (3) Depression Adjective Checklists (DACLs); (4) Minnesota Multiphasic Personality Inventory Depression Scale (MMPI-D); (5) Self-Rating Depression Scale (SDS); (6) Profile of Mood States (POMS); (7) Visual Analog Scale; (8) Hamilton Rating Scale (HRS); (9) Schedule for Affective Disorders and Schizophrenia (SADS); (10) Diagnostic Interview Schedule (DIS); (11) Raskin Three Area Rating Scale; (12) Brief Psychiatric Rating Scale; (13)

Feelings and Concerns Checklist (FCCL); (14) Social Adjustment Scale; and (15) Hopkins Psychiatric Rating Scale. 1 figure. 2 tables. 184 references.

1.313. Reicherts, Michael, Sepp Käslin, Fritz Scheurer, Jörg Fleischhauer and Meinrad Perrez. "Depressed People Coping with Loss and Failure." Chapter in **Stress, Coping, and Health: A Situation-Behavior Approach Theory, Methods, Applications**, by Meinrad Perrez and Michael Reicherts, 113-123. Seattle, WA: Hogrefe and Huber, 1992.

1.314. Reilly, Thomas. "Differential Diagnosis of Anxiety and Depression." Chapter in **Testing Adults: A Reference Guide for Special Psychodiagnostic Assessments**, edited by Dennis P. Swiercinsky, 10-19. Kansas City, MO: Test Corporation of America, 1985.

1.315. Rice, F. Philip. "Depression." in **The Adolescent: Development, Relationships, and Culture**, Third Edition, by F. Philip Rice, 219-220. Boston, MA: Allyn and Bacon, 1981.

1.316. Risby, Emile D., S. Craig Risch and Alan Stoudemire. "Mood Disorders." in **Clinical Psychiatry for Medical Students**, edited by Alan Stoudemire, 157-198. Philadelphia, PA: J.B. Lippincott Company, 1990.

1.317. Rivers, P. Clayton. "Depression and Substance Abuse." in **Alcoholism and Substance Abuse in Special Populations**, edited by Gary W. Lawson and Ann W. Lawson, 38-45. Rockville, MD: Aspen Publishers, 1989.

1.318. Robinson, Marian D. "Manic Depression." in **Meaningful Counseling: A Guide for Students, Counselors, and Clergy**, by Marian D. Robinson, 90-93. New York, NY: Human Sciences Press, 1988.

The fantasies of the depressed person are grotesque and threatening. Imagery which does not correspond to this person's real past actions leads to despair. Ideas about failure, error, and sin preoccupy the depressed individual. Depression is a way of coping with inward turmoil.

1.319. Romeo, Felicia F. "Depression." in **Understanding Anorexia Nervosa**, by Felicia F. Romeo, 41. Springfield, IL: Charles C. Thomas, 1986.

There are significant differences between depressed individuals and persons afflicted with anorexia nervosa. The depressive is not proud about weight loss; the anorexic is proud. The depressive constantly makes self-deprecating statements; the anorexic makes such statements primarily relating to weight gain. The depressive loses the capacity to work; the anorexic does not lose this capacity. According to the Minnesota Multiphase Personality Test, however, it is possible for depression and anorexia nervosa to co-exist.

1.320. Root, Maria P.P., Patricia Fallon and William N. Friedrich. "Women and Depression." in **Bulimia: A Systems Approach to Treatment**, by Maria P.P. Root, Patricia Fallon and William N. Friedrich, 22-23. New York, NY: W.W. Norton and Company, 1986.

1.321. Rosenblatt, Seymour and Reynolds Dodson. "More Depression." Chapter in **Beyond Valium: The Brave New World of Psychochemistry**, by Seymour Rosenblatt and Reynolds Dodson, 102-117. New York, NY: G.P. Putnam's Sons, 1981.

Emil Kraepelin, a nineteenth-century taxonomist, differentiated between manic-depression and schizophrenia, proposing that manic-depression was an adjunct of common depression. There were similar thought patterns in manic-depression and schizophrenia. In the former condition, however, there was a cyclical aspect. Bipolar depression is a much more recent term used to refer to manic-depression. There is an implication of two opposing mood states. Regular depression is characterized as unipolar.

1.322. Rossi, A. Michael, Thomas F. Babor, Roger E. Meyer and Jack H. Mendelson. "Depression." in **The Use of Marihuana: A Psychological and Physiological Inquiry**, edited by Jack H. Mendelson, A. Michael Rossi and Roger E. Meyer, 122-123. New York, NY: Plenum, 1974.

1.323. Rubin, Theodore I. "Depression." in **Compassion and Self-Hate: An Alternative to Despair**, by Theodore I Rubin, 45-46. New York, NY: Ballantine Books, 1975.

Depression, a sign of self-hate and a negative way of discharging accumulated anger, sometimes prevents depressed persons from committing suicide. Depression robs these people of initiative, rendering them incapable of action. Depressed individuals have typically for years imposed upon themselves impossible standards.

1.324. Rubin, Theodore Isaac. "Depression." in **The Angry Book**, by Theodore Isaac Rubin, 52-53. New York, NY: Collier Books, 1969.

1.325. Russianoff, Penelope. "Depression: Breaking the Black Mood." Chapter in **When Am I Going to Be Happy?: How to Break the Emotional Bad Habits that Make You Miserable**, by Penelope Russianoff, 175-191. New York, NY: Bantam Books, 1988.

Dr. Penelope Russianoff was at the University of Michigan the year before World War II began. Twelve students attempted suicide during this time. Nine attempts were successful. Immediately after Pearl Harbor, there were no suicide attempts at this campus. A historical event - Pearl Harbor - put purpose into the lives of Americans, especially young Americans. An absence of purpose is a reason for suicidal depression.

1.326. Rutter, D.R. "Depressed Patients." in **Looking and Seeing: The Role of Visual Communication in Social Interaction**, by D.R. Rutter, 21-30. Chichester, England: John Wiley and Sons, 1984.

1.327. Rycroft, Charles. "Depression and Grief." in **Anxiety and Neurosis**, by Charles Rycroft, 47-49. Harmondsworth, England: Penguin, 1970.

1.328. Rycroft, Charles. "Guilt and Depression." in **Anxiety and Neurosis**, by Charles Rycroft, 44-47. Harmondsworth, England: Penguin, 1970.

Some people have the delusional idea they have committed a crime. These individuals experience depression, guilt, and anxiety. Some of these depressives have to be hospitalized because of suicidal ideation. The belief they have contributed through neglect to the death of a relative makes the delusional idea more plausible to them. These persons boast about their extraordinary sinfulness, believing incorrectly that hostile internal images in the mind are synonymous with action.

1.329. Rycroft, Charles. "Neurotic Depression." in **Anxiety and Neurosis**, by Charles Rycroft, 49-50. Harmondsworth, England: Penguin, 1970.

1.330. Rycroft, Charles. "Neurotic Depression." in **Anxiety and Neurosis**, by Charles Rycroft, 115-116. Harmondsworth, England: Penguin, 1970.

1.331. Salzman, Leon. "Depression." in **Developments in Psychoanalysis,** by Leon Salzman, 222-232. New York, NY: Grune and Stratton, 1962.

1.332. Sanford, Fillmore H. and Lawrence S. Wrightsman, Jr. "Depressive Reaction." in **Psychology: A Scientific Study of Man,** Third Edition, by Fillmore H. Sanford and Lawrence S. Wrightsman, Jr., 579. Belmont, CA: Brooks/Cole, 1970.

1.333. Sanford, Linda Tschirhart and Mary Ellen Donovan. "From Not Feeling Good about Ourselves to Not Feeling at All: Emotional Expression versus Depression." Chapter in **Women and Self-Esteem: Understanding and Improving the Way We Think and Feel about Ourselves,** by Linda Tschirhart Sanford and Mary Ellen Donovan, 353-368. Garden City, NY: Anchor Press/Doubleday, 1984.

1.334. Saul, Leon J. "Agitated Depression." in **Bases of Human Behavior: A Biologic Approach to Psychiatry,** by Leon J. Saul, 69. Philadelphia, PA: J.B. Lippincott Company, 1951. Reprint. Westport, CT: Greenwood Press, 1972.

Persons experiencing agitated depression usually have suppressed powerful hostilities. Conflicts occur between the hostilities and the conscience. These persons blame themselves for supposedly having engaged in one or more terrible wrongdoings. The wrongdoings are usually greatly exaggerated.

1.335. Saul, Leon J. "Depressions and Manic-Depressive Reactions." in **Bases of Human Behavior: A Biologic Approach to Psychiatry,** by Leon J. Saul, 69-72. Philadelphia, PA: J.B. Lippincott Company, 1951. Reprint. Westport CT: Greenwood Press, 1972.

The individual experiencing a manic attack can, in part, be described as someone with great inner drive, much initiative, and a sense of elation. This person is also constantly active, ultrasociable, and generally unrepressed. A manic attack defends the individual against depression and protects this person from the power of the conscience. The conscience is very prominent in depression.

1.336. Sayers, Janet. "Depression and Loss." Chapter in **Mothers of Psychoanalysis: Helene Deutsch, Karen Horney, Anna Freud and Melanie Klein,** by Janet Sayers, 232-237. New York, NY: W.W. Norton and Company, 1991.

1.337. Schaef, Anne Wilson. "Depression." in **When Society Becomes an Addict**, by Anne Wilson Schaef, 44-45. San Francisco: CA: Harper and Row, 1987.

1.338. Schafer, Roy. "Pathological Emotional States: The Example of Depression." in **A New Language for Psychoanalysis**, by Roy Schafer, 349-351. New Haven, CT: Yale University Press, 1976.

1.339. Schuster, Clara S. "Delayed Depression (Nonpsychotic Postpartum Depression)." in **The Process of Human Development: A Holistic Life-Span Approach**, Third Edition, by Clara Shaw Schuster and Shirley Smith Ashburn, 675-677. Philadelphia, PA: J.B. Lippincott Company, 1992.

Several weeks or months after delivery, 25% to 50% of mothers experience depression. Fear of the baby's death, panic attacks, and crying are a few of the behaviors which may accompany depression at this time. Mothers who had drug or alcohol abuse problems before the arrival of their child may now find coping with life even more difficult than before. Fantasies associated with pregnancy do not coincide with the realities of raising the baby. A year or more may pass before a woman redefines herself as a mother.

1.340. Schuster, Clara S. "Depression During the First Week ('Postpartum Blues')." in **The Process of Human Development: A Holistic Life-Span Approach**, Third Edition, by Clara Shaw Schuster and Shirley Smith Ashburn, 674-675. Philadelphia, PA: J.B. Lippincott Company, 1992.

Between 50% and 84% of mothers experience some degree of sadness the first week, after the birth of their child. Irritability, headache, and insomnia sometimes accompany this sadness. Rapidly decreasing levels, after delivery, of estrogen and progesterone may also help explain this depression. Maternal sleep deprivation, due to movement of the baby, may help account in explaining postpartum blues.

1.341. Schuster, Clara S. "Psychotic Depression." in **The Process of Human Development: A Holistic Life-Span Approach**, Third Edition, by Clara Shaw Schuster and Shirley Smith Ashburn, 677. Philadelphia, PA: J.B. Lippincott Company, 1992.

Although true puerperal psychosis is rare, severe irritability, paranoia, and hallucinations may characterize it, when it does occur. Mothers afflicted with this condition must receive counseling.

1.342. Schwenk, Thomas L. and James C. Coyne. "Depression." Chapter in **Textbook of Family Practice**, Fourth Edition, edited by Robert E. Rakel, 1582-1595. Philadelphia, PA: W.B. Saunders, 1990.

Seventy-five is the age at which depressed men are most likely to commit suicide; depressed women are most likely to commit suicide between age fifty-five and sixty-five. The never-married depressed person is at highest risk for suicide; the married person with children is at lowest risk. Depressed unemployed persons have a higher suicide rate than do their employed counterparts. Suicide is also more likely in the person who is physically ill, is an alcoholic, or has a history of prior attempts. 8 tables. 1 figure. 44 references.

1.343. Scully, James H. and Steven L. Dubovsky. "Depression." in **Medicine: Diagnosis and Treatment**, edited by Robert W. Schrier, 487-489. Boston, MA: Little, Brown and Company, 1988.

Hyperthyroidism, hypothyroidism, porphyria, pernicious anemia, multiple sclerosis, and pneumonia are examples of medical illnesses that can cause depression. The sleep electroencephalogram is the most reliable biological test for depression. Electroconvulsive therapy (ECT) is the safest and most effective antidepressant treatment. If a patient fails to respond to an antidepressant, the prescribed dose may be inadequate, consumption of alcohol may be increasing the metabolism of the antidepressant, or - a third example - the patient may not be taking the medication. 2 tables.

1.344. Semrud-Clikeman, Margaret. "Assessment of Childhood Depression." Chapter in **Handbook of Psychological and Educational Assessment of Children: Personality, Behavior, and Context**, edited by Cecil R. Reynolds and Randy W. Kamphaus, 279-297. New York, NY: Guilford Press, 1990.

A number of self-report scales are used to assess childhood depression. One is the Children's Depression Inventory (CDI), which evolved from the Beck Depression Inventory (BDI). The Short Children's Depression Inventory is based on the Short Beck Depression Inventory. The Children's Depression Scale (CDS) is another self-report scale. R.B. Sherick created the Hopelessness Scale and P. Birleson created the Depression Self-Rating Scale (DSRS). All these psychometric instruments differ, in a variety of ways, on how to assess childhood depression. Author biographical information. 105 references.

1.345. Shaffer, Laurance F. "Manic-Depressive Psychosis." in **Fields of Psychology: Basic and Applied**, Second Edition, edited by J.P. Guildford, 318-321. Toronto, ON: D. Van Nostrand, 1950.

Manic-depressive psychosis, an illness of emotional extremes, was, until about fifty years ago, viewed as two separate illnesses. Most individuals, who have this illness and are, for the first time, admitted to a hospital, are between forty and fifty years of age. The attention of these persons in the manic state is flighty. They talk and act at random; sleep little; and very rarely have delusions of persecution or grandeur. Neither metabolism, glandular disorders, nor changes in the brain have convincingly accounted for manic-depressive psychosis.

1.346. Shipley, Kenneth. "Depression." in **Interviewing and Counseling in Communicative Disorders: Principles and Procedures**, by Kenneth Shipley, 199-200. New York, NY: Macmillan, 1992.

Depression is the fourth stage of Dr. Elisabeth Kübler-Ross's grieving process.

1.347. Siegel, Martha. "Depression." Chapter in **The Management of Common Human Miseries: A Text for Primary Health Care Practitioners**, edited by Bonnie Bullough, 367-384. New York, NY: Springer, 1979.

Depression is related to loss - loss of money, loss of status, loss of health - and can last for years. Fatigue and pain are usually associated with depression. The depressed person may have difficulty falling asleep, may frequently awaken, or may wake up earlier than usual. He or she may postpone daily tasks pertaining to personal hygiene. The depressed individual may also be indecisive and introspective. 2 tables. 20 references.

1.348. Siegman, Aron Wolfe. "Vocal Correlates of Anger and Depression." in **Nonverbal Behavior and Communication**, edited by Aron W. Siegman and Stanley Feldstein, 214-216. Hillsdale, NJ: Lawrence Erlbaum Associates, 1978.

1.349. Siegman, Aron Wolfe. "Vocal Correlates of Depression." in **Multichannel Integrations of Nonverbal Behavior**, edited by Aron W. Siegman and Stanley Feldstein, 48-52. Hillsdale, NJ: Lawrence Erlbaum Associates, 1985.

A slow rate of speech, decreased mutual gazing, social withdrawal, and a reduced level of energy are some of the characteristics of depressed persons.

1.350. Siever, Larry J., Kenneth L. Davis and Lauren Kantor Gorman. "Pathogenesis of Mood Disorders." Chapter in **Foundations of Psychiatry,** edited by Kenneth Davis, Howard Klar and Joseph T. Coyle, 254-262. Philadelphia, PA: W.B. Saunders, 1991.

1.351. Silverman, Robert E. "Causes of Depression." in **Psychology,** Fourth Edition, by Robert E. Silverman, 466-468. Englewood Cliffs, NJ: Prentice-Hall, 1982.

1.352. Silverstone, Trevor and Paul Turner. "Depressive Illness." in **Drug Treatment in Psychiatry,** by Trevor Silverstone and Paul Turner, 102-103. London: Routledge and Kegan Paul, 1974.

1.353. Silverstone, Trevor and Paul Turner. "Depressive Reaction." in **Drug Treatment in Psychiatry,** by Trevor Silverstone and Paul Turner, 103. London: Routledge and Kegan Paul, 1974.

1.354. Silverstone, Trevor and Paul Turner. "Mania." in **Drug Treatment in Psychiatry,** by Trevor Silverstone and Paul Turner, 103. London: Routledge and Kegan Paul, 1974.

1.355. Simon, Gregory E. "Screening for Depression." in **Outpatient Medicine,** edited by Stephan D. Fihn and Steven R. McGee, 587-588. Philadelphia, PA: W.B. Saunders, 1992.

The Beck Depression Inventory, Hopkins Symptom Checklist Depression Scale, and Center for Epidemiologic Studies Depression Scale (CES-D) are used to screen patients for depression. Loss of energy, crying spells, suicidal ideation, and other variables are measured by these research instruments. It is believed they are more effective in measuring depression than is a structured psychiatric interview. 2 references.

1.356. Siomopoulos, V. "Depression and Elation: Structural Mechanisms." in **The Structure of Psychopathological Experience,** by V. Siomopoulos, 68-70. New York, NY: Brunner/Mazel, 1983.

1.357. Skinner, B.F. "Depression." in **Science and Human Behavior**, by B.F. Skinner, 362-363. New York, NY: Macmillan, 1953.

1.358. Smith, Robert E. and George Winokur. "Affective Disorders." Chapter in **The Child at Psychiatric Risk**, edited by Ralph E. Tarter, 228-244. New York, NY: Oxford University Press, 1983.

1.359. Snider, Arthur J. "Psychiatrists Fear Epidemic of Depression and Hopelessness." in **Psychology: Its Principles and Meanings**, by Lyle E. Bourne, Jr. and Bruce R. Ekstrand, 360. Hinsdale, IL: Dryden Press, 1973.

Drs. Jan Fawcett and Harold Visotsky are psychiatrists who were quoted in the **Chicago Daily News** in 1972.

1.360. Snyder, C.R., Raymond L. Higgins and Rita J. Stucky. "Depression and Excuses." in **Excuses: Masquerades in Search of Grace**, by C.R. Snyder, Raymond L. Higgins and Rita J. Stucky, 230-237. New York, NY: John Wiley and Sons, 1983.

1.361. Solomon, Joel. "Alcoholism and Affective Disorders: Methodological Considerations." Chapter in **Alcoholism and Clinical Psychiatry**, edited by Joel Solomon, 81-85. New York, NY: Plenum, 1982.

1.362. Storandt, Martha. "Depression." in **Clinical Geriatrics**, Third Edition, edited by Isadore Rossman, 612-613. Philadelphia, PA: J.B. Lippincott Company, 1986.

Suicide notes indicate that health or loneliness is the reason for suicide by elderly persons; rejection in love is the reason for suicide by young or middle-aged adults. The Zung Self-Rating Depression Scale and the Beck Depression Inventory (BDI) are used to measure severity of depression. 1 figure.

1.363. Storr, Anthony. "Aggression in Relation to Depression." Chapter in **Human Aggression**, by Anthony Storr, 72-81. New York, NY: Atheneum, 1969.

Aspects of depression and aggression can be noted in animals, such as snakes and geese. If a goose accidentally loses a mate, the goose which has the experience of loss will become apathetic, and will exhibit a different posture. Efforts to arouse this goose's aggression will not be successful. If this goose can compete again, it may violently attack another goose. The attacking goose will then recover its normal posture and behavior. This illustrates the aggressive drive is severely inhibited in depressed animals. 2 references.

1.364. Straus, Erwin W. "Disorders of Personal Time in Depressive States." Chapter in **Phenomenological Psychology**, translated, in part, by Erling Eng, 290-295. New York, NY: Basic Books, 1966.

1.365. Suomi, Stephen J. and Harry F. Harlow. "Production and Alleviation of Depressive Behaviors in Monkeys." in **Psychopathology: Experimental Models**, edited by Jack D. Maser and Martin E.P. Seligman, 131-173. San Francisco, CA: W.H. Freeman and Company, 1977.

1.366. Taylor, W.S. "Manic-Depressive Psychosis." in **Dynamic and Abnormal Psychology**, by W.S. Taylor, 590-596. New York, NY: American Book Company, 1954.

1.367. Teri, Linda and Burton V. Reifler. "Depression and Dementia." Chapter in **Handbook of Clinical Gerontology**, Pergamon General Psychology Series 146, by Laura L. Carstensen and Barry A. Edelstein, 112-119. New York, NY: Pergamon, 1987.

1.368. Thomas, R. Murray. "Correlates and Causes of Depression." in **Counseling and Life-Span Development**, by R. Murray Thomas, 312-313. Newbury Park, CA: Sage, 1990.

There does not appear to be a single cause of depression. Depression can be caused by biological and other factors. Shortage in the brain of a chemical substance, norepinephrine, can bring about depression. Drugs that increase norepinephrine, when administered to depressed individuals, can often alleviate this condition. Retirement, death of a spouse, and financial insecurity can precipitate depression, which can, in turn, precipitate suicide.

1.369. Thomas, R. Murray. "Depression, Loneliness, and Lack of Incentive to Live." in **Counseling and Life-Span Development**, by R. Murray Thomas, 311-312. Newbury Park, CA: Sage, 1990.

Depressed elderly individuals often feel they have wasted their lives, believing they have not accomplished anything of value. These persons also feel existence is futile. For males in the U.S., the older the males, the higher the suicide rate, especially after age sixty-five. For females, the suicide rate peaks at approximately age forty-five. White males have higher suicide rates than black males or black females.

1.370. Tiger, Lionel. "The Pressure of Depression." in **The Pursuit of Pleasure**, by Lionel Tiger, 254-256. Boston, MA: Little, Brown and Company, 1992.

1.371. Tolor, Alexander and Herbert C. Schulberg. "Manic-Depressive Functioning on the Bender-Gestalt." in **An Evaluation of the Bender-Gestalt Test**, by Alexander Tolor and Herbert C. Schulberg, 101-103. Springfield, IL: Charles C. Thomas, 1963.

1.372. Trower, Peter, Andrew Casey and Windy Dryden. "Depression." Chapter in **Cognitive-Behavioural Counselling in Action**, by Peter Trower, Andrew Casey and Windy Dryden, 122-134. London: Sage, 1988.

Categories of symptoms of depression and one example for each category: (1) motivational (apathy), (2) affective (guilt), (3) behavioral (decreased activity), (4) cognitive (negative thinking), and (5) biological (loss of appetite). 2 figures.

1.373. Tucker, Irving F. "Depression." in **Adjustment: Models and Mechanisms**, by Irving F. Tucker, 367-368. New York, NY: Academic Press, 1970.

1.374. Van Dyke, Craig and Richard J. Goldberg. "Depression." in **Review of General Psychiatry**, Third Edition, edited by Howard H. Goldman, 456. Norwalk, CT: Appleton and Lange, 1992.

It is easy to both overdiagnose and underdiagnose depression. Sleep disturbances, appetite disturbance, fatigue, and impaired concentration may be due to depression. However, they may be due to other conditions. Fatigue may be due to anemia and pain may be the cause of sleep disturbances.

1.375. Vickery, Donald M. and James F. Fries. "Depression." in **Take Care of Yourself: Your Personal Guide to Self-Care and Preventing Illness**, Fourth Edition, by Donald M. Vickery and James F. Fries, 69-70. Reading, MA: Addison-Wesley, 1989.

1.376. Warga, Richard G. "Depressive Neurosis." in **Personal Awareness: A Psychology of Adjustment,** by Richard G. Warga, 417. Boston, MA: Houghton Mifflin, 1974.

1.377. Weary, Gifford. "Depression and Sensitivity to Social Information." Chapter in **Affect and Social Behavior,** edited by Bert S. Moore and Alice M. Isen, 207-230. Cambridge: Cambridge University Press, 1990.

1.378. Weekes, Claire. "Depression." Chapter in **Hope and Help for Your Nerves,** by Claire Weekes, 134-144. New York, NY: Bantam Books, 1969.

1.379. Weingartner, Herbert and Douglas Herrmann. "Cognitive Failures in Depression: Failures in Effort-Demanding Cognitive Processes." in **Memory Improvement: Implications for Memory Theory,** edited by Douglas J. Herrmann, Herbert Weingartner, Alan Searleman and Cathy McEvoy, 24-25. New York, NY: Springer-Verlag, 1992.

1.380. Wekstein, Louis. "Depressive Reactions." in **Handbook of Suicidology: Principles, Problems, and Practice,** by Louis Wekstein, 83-85. New York, NY: Brunner/Mazel, 1979.

1.381. Wenrich, W.W. "Depressive Reaction." in **A Primer of Behavior Modification,** by W.W. Wenrich, 79. Belmont, CA: Brooks/Cole, 1970.

1.382. Whitman, R. Douglas. "Depression." in **Adjustment: The Development and Organization of Human Behavior,** by R. Douglas Whitman, 217-221. New York, NY: Oxford University Press, 1980.

1.383. Wicks, Robert J. "Physical Causes of Depression." in **Helping Others: Ways of Listening, Sharing and Counseling,** by Robert J. Wicks, 109-110. Radnor, PA: Chilton Book Company, 1979.

1.384. Wicks, Robert J. "Signs of Depression." in **Helping Others: Ways of Listening, Sharing and Counseling,** by Robert J. Wicks, 106-109. Radnor, PA: Chilton Book Company, 1979.

Depression and physical ailments - headaches, stomachaches, cold symptoms - often coexist in the same person. Early morning awakening can be another sign of depression. A person goes to bed, wakes up, for example, at approximately 3:00 A.M., then tosses and turns, instead of falling asleep. A change in eating habits can also be a sign of depression.

1.385. Wicks, Robert J. "Who Gets Depressed?" in **Helping Others: Ways of Listening, Sharing and Counseling,** by Robert J. Wicks, 105-106. Radnor, PA: Chilton Book Company, 1979.

Competition to qualify for admission to college in Japan and Germany is very stressful. Nonqualifying students sometimes see suicide as the alternative to not qualifying for admission. Neither wealth nor status nor power is a guarantee against depression. Winston Churchill was repeatedly depressed. Abraham Lincoln also used to experience depression. He feared that if he carried a gun he might commit suicide.

1.386. Winnicott, D.W. "The Value of Depression." in **Home Is Where We Start from: Essays by a Psychoanalyst,** compiled and edited by Clare Winnicott, Ray Shepherd and Madeleine Davis, 71-79. Harmondsworth: Penguin, 1986.

"The Value of Depression" was originally a paper presented at a general meeting, Association of Psychiatric Social Workers, September 1963.

1.387. Winship, Elizabeth C. "Moods, Depression, and Suicide." Chapter in **Reaching Your Teenager,** by Elizabeth C. Winship, 210-222. Boston, MA: Houghton Mifflin, 1983.

Some causes of depression in teenagers: (1) traits in teenagers that teenagers also see in their parents and despise; (2) use by parents of extreme shame and punishment to raise their children; (3) overly protective and overly directive parents; and (4) use of children by parents to fulfill parental unachieved goals.

1.388. Wisocki, Patricia A. "Depression." in **Behavior Modification with Women,** edited by Elaine A. Blechman, 462-463. New York, NY: Guilford Press, 1984.

Depressive symptoms such as physical complaints, suspiciousness, irritability, delusions, and apathy are more commonly noted in elderly subjects than in younger subjects. Younger subjects reveal more guilt. Estrogens inhibit monoamine oxidase and alleviate depressive symptoms in menopausal women.

Monoamine oxidase is an enzyme which has been implicated in causing depression.

1.389. Wolfe, Janet L. "Depression and Low Confidence." in **Clinical Applications of Rational-Emotive Therapy,** edited by Albert Ellis and Michael E. Bernard, 108-109. New York, NY: Plenum, 1985.

1.390. Wolman, Benjamin B. "Depressive Disorders." in **Handbook of States of Consciousness,** edited by Benjamin B. Wolman and Montague Ullman, 327-329. New York, NY: Van Nostrand Reinhold, 1986.

1.391. Zetzel, Elizabeth R. "Depression and the Incapacity to Bear It." in **Drives, Affects, Behavior,** Volume 2, Essays in Memory of Marie Bonaparte, edited by Max Schur, 243-274. New York, NY: International Universities Press, 1965.

1.392. Zimbardo, Philip G. "Affective Disorders." in **Psychology and Life,** Twelfth Edition, by Philip G. Zimbardo, 536-539. Glenview, IL: Scott, Foresman and Company, 1988.

A teenager attempts suicide every nine minutes and succeeds every ninety minutes. One thousand teenagers attempt suicide weekly; 125 succeed. The U.S. suicide rate among teenagers has increased 300% during the last twenty years. The main predictor of female youth suicide is depression. Conduct disorders/drug abuse are usually associated with male youth suicide. Inner turmoil, external distress, shame, and guilt contribute to these suicides. 1 table. 2 photographs.

GOVERNMENT DOCUMENTS AND ASSOCIATION PUBLICATIONS

1.393. Cappeliez, Philippe. **Depression, Loneliness and Grief among the Elderly,** Writings in Gerontology 10: Mental Health and Aging, Ottawa, ON: National Advisory Council on Aging, 1991.

1.394. DeLisi, Lynn E. Editor. **Depression in Schizophrenia.** Washington, DC: American Psychiatric Press, 1990.

A symposium was held during the Annual Meeting, American Psychiatric Association, May 1986. This seven-chapter book is based on the proceedings of that meeting. Thomas Barnes,

Alec Roy, Keith L. Rogers, and Timothy J. Crow are four examples of authors included in this publication.

1.395. Keitner, Gabor I. Editor. **Depression and Families: Impact and Treatment.** Washington, DC: American Psychiatric Press, 1990.

1.396. Lobel, Brana and Robert M.A. Hirschfeld. **Depression: What We Know.** Rockville, MD: National Institute of Mental Health, 1985. DHHS Publication No. (ADM) 85-1318.

Asthma, diabetes, hyperthyroidism, hypothyroidism, multiple sclerosis, and syphilis are some of the physical illnesses associated with depression.

1.397. McGrath, Ellen, Gwendolyn Puryear Keita, Bonnie R. Strickland and Nancy Felipe Russo. **Women and Depression: Risk Factors and Treatment Issues: Final Report of the American Psychological Association's National Task Force on Women and Depression.** Washington, DC: American Psychological Association, 1990.

1.398. Miller, Andrew H. Editor. **Depressive Disorders and Immunity.** Washington, DC: American Psychiatric Press, 1989.

The American Psychiatric Association held in Chicago, Illinois its 1986 annual meeting. A symposium on depressive disorders and immunity was held at this meeting. A book consisting of eight chapters, authored by twenty contributors, was based on the symposium. The focus of this book is on affective disorders and the immune system.

1.399. Othmer, Ekkehard and Sieglinde C. Othmer. **Life on a Roller Coaster: Coping with the Ups and Downs of Mood Disorders.** Washington, DC: PIA Press, 1989.

1.400. Shafii, Mohammad and Sharon Lee Shafii. Editors. **Biological Rhythms, Mood Disorders, Light Therapy, and the Pineal Gland.** Washington, DC: American Psychiatric Press, 1990.

1.401. U.S. Department of Health and Human Services. Public Health Service. Agency for Health Care Policy and Research. **Depression in Primary Care: Detection, Diagnosis,**

and Treatment, Quick Reference Guide for Clinicians, Number 5. Rockville, MD: U.S. Department of Health and Human Services. Public Health Service. Agency for Health Care Policy and Research, April 1993. AHCPR Publication No. 93-0552.

1.402. U.S. Department of Health and Human Services. Public Health Service. Agency for Health Care Policy and Research. **Depression in Primary Care: Volume 1. Detection and Diagnosis,** Clinical Practice Guideline, Number 5, Rockville, MD: U.S. Department of Health and Human Services. Public Health Service. Agency for Health Care Policy and Research, April 1993. AHCPR Publication No. 93-0550.

1.403. U.S. Department of Health and Human Services. Public Health Service. Agency for Health Care Policy and Research. **Depression in Primary Care: Volume 2. Treatment of Major Depression.** Clinical Practice Guideline, Number 5, Rockville, MD: U.S. Department of Health and Human Services. Public Health Service. Agency for Health Care Policy and Research, April 1993. AHCPR Publication No. 93-0551.

1.404. U.S. Department of Health and Human Services. Public Health Service. Agency for Health Care Policy and Research. **Depression Is a Treatable Illness: A Patient's Guide,** Clinical Practice Guideline, Rockville, MD: U.S. Department of Health and Human Services. Public Health Service. Agency for Health Care Policy and Research, April 1993. AHCPR Publication No. 93-0553.

CHAPTERS AND SECTIONS IN GOVERNMENT DOCUMENTS AND ASSOCIATION PUBLICATIONS

1.405. McEwan, Kimberley L., Martha Donnelly, Duncan Robertson and Clyde Hertzman. "Depression." in **Mental Health Problems among Canada's Seniors: Demographic and Epidemiologic Considerations,** by Kimberley L. McEwan, Martha Donnelly, Duncan Robertson and Clyde Hertzman, 17-19. Ottawa, ON: Department of National Health and Welfare, 1991.

The five provinces in Canada with the highest estimated depression cases for 1986 (in descending order): (1) Ontario (95, 299), (2) Quebec (62,458), (3) British Columbia (33,552), (4) Alberta (18,365), and (5) Manitoba (12,854). The Yukon (territory) had the lowest number of estimated depression cases (86). 2 tables.

1.406. Waldinger, Robert J. "Mood Disorders." Chapter in **Psychiatry for Medical Students**, Second Edition, by Robert J. Waldinger, 103-143. Washington, DC: American Psychiatric Press, 1990.

Examples of symptoms of depression: (1) affective (anhedonia), (2) vegetative (sleep disturbance), (3) motivational (suicidal thoughts), (4) cognitive (guilt), and (5) somatic (bodily complaints). Examples of what to bear in mind when evaluating a depressed person: (1) medical history, (2) physical examination, (3) complete blood count (CBC), (4) blood chemistries, (5) thyroid function, (6) urinalysis, (7) chest x-ray, and (8) electrocardiogram (EKG). Examples of indicators a depressed person should be hospitalized: (1) when there is a significant risk of suicide and/or homicide, (2) when the ability to care for oneself has been lost, and (3) when the depression has caused life-threatening acute medical conditions, for example, anorexia. 10 tables. 19 references.

1.407. World Health Organization. "Mood [Affective] Disorders." in **The ICD-10 Classification of Mental and Behavioural Disorders: Clinical Descriptions and Diagnostic Guidelines**, by World Health Organization, 110-131. Geneva: World Health Organization, 1992.

CONFERENCES, MEETINGS, SEMINARS, SYMPOSIA, AND WORKSHOPS

1.408. Cole, Jonathan O., Alan F. Schatzberg and Shervert H. Frazier. Editors. **Depression: Biology, Psychodynamics, and Treatment.** New York, NY: Plenum, 1978.

Proceedings of a symposium on depression, sponsored by McLean Hospital in Belmont, Massachusetts, held on March 28, 1976. There were twenty-three contributors to this symposium.

1.409. Ingram, Rick E. Editor. **Contemporary Psychological Approaches to Depression: Theory, Research, and Treatment.** New York, NY: Plenum, 1990.

Eleven chapters authored by twenty-one contributors to the Proceedings of the First Annual Conference on Contemporary Psychological Approaches to Depression: Treatment, Research, and Theory - from a Conference Series on Contemporary Issues in Clinical Psychology, February 6-7, 1988, San Diego, California. Lauren B. Alloy, Mark D. Evans, Constance Hammen, Mary J. Naus, and Brian F. Shaw were a few of the contributors.

1.410. Mendlewicz, J. Editor. **New Advances in the Diagnosis and Treatment of Depressive Illness,** Proceedings of the Fifteenth International Congress of Therapeutics, Part Three, Brussels, Belgium, September 5-9, 1979, Amsterdam: Excerpta Medica, 1980.

There are ten papers. W.E. Bunney, Jr., B.J. Carroll, J.P. Desager, and H.E. Hansen are examples of authors who attended the congress. The focus of papers ranged from cardiovascular toxicity and amitriptyline in rabbits to the typology of depressive states.

1.411. Mendlewicz, J., A. Cooper and H.M. van Praag. Editors. **Depressive Illness: Biological and Psychopharmacological Issues,** Advances in Biological Psychiatry, Volume 7, Basel: S. Karger, 1981.

The Interdisciplinary Society of Biological Psychiatry and the World Psychiatric Association (WPA) held its first joint meeting in Amsterdam, Netherlands, September 11-12, 1980. European and American investigators contributed eighteen papers. Pharmacology, neurobiochemistry, and endocrinology were some of the subject areas on which papers were based. "Sulpiride, Psychosis, and Mood" (P. Borenstein and F. Gekiere) is an example of one of the papers presented. "Lithium and Antidepressants in the Prophylaxis of Depression" (I. Glen) is a second example of a presented paper.

1.412. Scott, John Paul and Edward C. Senay. Editors. **Separation and Depression: Clinical and Research Aspects,** American Association for the Advancement of Science, Publication Number 94, Washington, DC: American Association for the Advancement of Science, 1973.

Symposium participants met in Chicago, Illinois on December 27, 1970 to discuss separation and depression. Twelve papers were later published. Separation in dogs and monkeys was a major area of discussion. Another major area of discussion was separation in human clinical practice. John M. Stewart, Harry F. Harlow, Thomas H. Holmes, and Eugene S. Paykel were four authors who attended this symposium.

PARTS OF CONFERENCES, MEETINGS, SEMINARS, SYMPOSIA, AND WORKSHOPS

1.413. Barry, Herbert, III. "Alcoholism and Depression." in **Substance Abuse and Psychiatric Illness: Proceedings of the Second Annual Coatesville-Jefferson Conference on Addiction,**

edited by Edward Gottheil, A. Thomas McLellan and Keith A. Druley, 69-70. New York, NY: Pergamon, 1980.

1.414. Berreman, Charles H., Edward B. Blanchard, Jerry M. Suls, Shirley P. Schwarz, Lisa Scharff and Barbara Greene. "Changes in Anxiety and Depression among Irritable Bowel Syndrome Patients Following Active Treatment, Attention Placebo and Wait-List Control." in **Twenty-First Annual Meeting, Association for Applied Psychophysiology and Biofeedback: Exploring the Future: New Frontiers in Biofeedback and Psychophysiology, Washington, DC, March 23-28, 1990**, 19-21. Wheat Ridge, CO: Association for Applied Psychophysiology and Biofeedback, 1990.

1.415. Berreman, Chuck, Edward B. Blanchard, Shirley P. Schwarz and Jerry Suls. "Anxiety, Depression, Assertiveness and Symptoms of Irritable Bowel Syndrome: A Correlational Study." in **Twentieth Annual Meeting, Association for Applied Psychophysiology and Biofeedback: Roots to the Future, San Diego, California, March 17-22, 1989**, 21-23. Wheat Ridge, CO: Association for Applied Psychophysiology and Biofeedback, 1989.

1.416. Davitz, Joel R. "Depression." in **Feelings and Emotions: The Loyola Symposium**, edited by Magda B. Arnold, 252-254. New York, NY: Academic Press, 1970.

1.417. Rapoport, Judith L. "Depressive Disorder." in **Psychopathology of Children and Youth: A Cross-Cultural Perspective, Report of a Conference**, edited by Elizabeth F. Purcell, 164-165. New York, NY: Josiah Macy, Jr. Foundation, 1980.

The expressions "masked depression" and "depressive equivalent" are not adequate diagnostic labels for defining depressive disorder in children. Genuine adult-type depression is rare in children.

REVIEW PAPERS

1.418. Allen, Martin G., Stephen Cohen, William Pollin and Stanley I. Greenspan. "Affective Illness in Veteran Twins: A Diagnostic Review." **American Journal of Psychiatry** 131 (November 1974): 1234-1239.

Data was obtained from the National Academy of Sciences (NASs)/National Research Council (NRC) Veteran Twin Registry, which consisted of nearly 16,000 computer records. These records pertained to pairs of twins born between 1917 and 1927. The twins had served in the U.S. Armed Forces. One or both twins had been diagnosed as psychotic, after entry on active duty. Analysis of data revealed a genetic component in affective illness. This paper was presented at the 127th Annual Meeting, American Psychiatric Association, Detroit, Michigan, May 6-10, 1974. Author biographical information. Abstract. 4 tables. 49 references.

1.419. Baldwin, R.C. "Late Life Depression and Structural Brain Changes: A Review of Recent Magnetic Resonance Imaging Research." **International Journal of Geriatric Psychiatry** 8 (February 1993): 115-123.

1.420. Barbee, Evelyn L. "African American Women and Depression: A Review and Critique of the Literature." **Archives of Psychiatric Nursing** 6 (October 1992): 257-265.

1.421. Beardslee, William R., Jules Bemporad, Martin B. Keller and Gerald L. Klerman. "Children of Parents with Major Affective Disorder: A Review." **American Journal of Psychiatry** 140 (July 1983): 825-832.

It is during early infancy and adolescence that children whose parents are afflicted with affective illness are particularly vulnerable, it seems, to develop psychopathology. Abstract. Author biographical information. 2 tables. 67 references.

1.422. Bunney, William E., Jr. and John M. Davis. "Norepinephrine in Depressive Reactions: A Review." **Archives of General Psychiatry** 13 (December 1965): 483-494.

1.423. Carroll, Bernard J., John M. Fielding and Timothy G. Blashki. "Depression Rating Scales: A Critical Review." **Archives of General Psychiatry** 28 (March 1973): 361-366.

The individuals studied were sixty-seven patients who were depressed and who were in three different settings. The patients were administered the Hamilton Rating Scale for Depression (HRS) and the Zung Self-Rating Depression Scale (SRS). Although the HRS distinguished the subgroups clearly - inpatient, day hospital, general practice - the SRS did not. Author biographical information. Abstract. 2 tables. 1 figure. 33 references.

1.424. Chodoff, Paul. "The Depressive Personality: A Critical Review." **Archives of General Psychiatry** 27 (November 1972): 666-673.

1.425. Coleman, Philip M. "Depression During the Female Climacteric Period." **Journal of Advanced Nursing** 18 (October 1993): 1540-1546.

The Roy Adaptation Model views the female climacteric period within a bio-psycho-social framework. This model, discussed by P. Aggleton and H. Chalmers in an article published in 1984 in **Nursing Times**, can form the basis for care provision for women in the climacteric-period stage of their lives. Author biographical information. Abstract. 45 references.

1.426. Costello, Charles G. "A Critical Review of Seligman's Laboratory Experiments on Learned Helplessness and Depression in Humans." **Journal of Abnormal Psychology** 87 (February 1978): 21-31.

After a critical review of six laboratory experiments by M.E.P. Seligman and colleagues, Charles G. Costello concludes there is little or no support in these experiments to support the learned helplessness theory of depression. Costello discusses seven methodological and conceptual problems in relation to Seligman's experiments. Author biographical information. Abstract. 1 reference note. 27 references.

1.427. Crook, Thomas and John Eliot. "Parental Death During Childhood and Adult Depression: A Critical Review of the Literature." **Psychological Bulletin** 87 (March 1980): 252-259.

Although parental death during childhood and depression during adulthood may be related, there is no firm empirical data to support the supposition that the death of one or both parents during childhood will predispose a surviving child to become depressed, due to loss or rejection experienced, when the child reaches adulthood. Author biographical information. Abstract. 29 references.

1.428. Freed, Earl X. "Alcohol and Mood: An Updated Review." **International Journal of the Addictions** 13 (February 1978): 173-200.

Nonalcoholics expect, after they drink, elevated moods and the ability to relax. This tends to occur. Alcoholics expect, after they drink, to experience a decrease in anxiety and depression. The reverse occurs. Author biographical information. 1 table. Acknowledgement. 130 references.

1.429. Friedman, Edward S., Duncan B. Clark and Samuel Gershon. "Stress, Anxiety, and Depression: Review of Biological, Diagnostic and Nosologic Issues." **Journal of Anxiety Disorders** 6 (October-December 1992): 337-363.

1.430. Gift, Audrey G. and Susan H. McCrone. "Depression in Patients with COPD." **Heart and Lung** 22 (July-August 1993): 289-297.

It is estimated that 42% of patients with COPD (chronic obstructive pulmonary disease) are depressed. Research instruments, including the MMPI (Minnesota Multiphasic Personality Inventory) and subscales of the Massachusetts Mental Health Center, revealed that persons with COPD have low self-esteem and avoid spontaneity. Some COPD patients have been helped rapidly and significantly with the aid of tricyclic antidepressants. However, bupropion (Wellbrutrin), fluoxetine (Prozac), and trazodone (Desyrel) have not been studied in these patients. Although electroconvulsive therapy (ECT) can be effective in depressed elderly patients, relapse is frequent and a maintenance program has to be established. The Life Review and Experience Form can help depressed older adults increase their life satisfaction. Author biographical information. Abstract. 67 references.

1.431. Herrmann, Manfred and claus-W. Wallesch. "Depressive Changes in Stroke Patients." **Disability and Rehabilitation** 15 (April-June 1993): 55-66.

1.432. Hill, Michael A. "Light, Circadian Rhythms, and Mood Disorders: A Review." **Annals of Clinical Psychiatry** 4 (June 1992): 131-146.

1.433. Jacobson, Alan M. "Depression and Diabetes." **Diabetes Care** 16 (December 1993): 1621-1623.

1.434. Kendell, R.E. "The Classification of Depressions: A Review of Contemporary Confusion." **British Journal of Psychiatry** 129 (July 1976): 15-28.

There are disputes and disagreement regarding what distinguishes depression from sadness, depressive illnesses from anxiety states, affective psychosis from schizophrenia, and recurrent depression from personality disorder. These are arbitrary and ill-defined. Many different classifications of depressive illness - with conflicting claims and methodological problems - have since 1926 been proposed. There are classifications of depression embracing from one to thirteen categories. 1 table. Acknowledgement. 47 references. Author biographical information.

1.435. Lamberty, Greg J. and Linas A. Bieliauskas. "Distinguishing between Depression and Dementia in the Elderly: A Review of Neuropsychological Findings." **Archives of Clinical Neuropsychology** 8 (March-April 1993): 149-170.

1.436. Lloyd, Camille. "Life Events and Depressive Disorder Reviewed. I. Events as Predisposing Factors." **Archives of General Psychiatry** 37 (May 1980): 529-535.

Hypothesis: life events during childhood/early adolescence may predispose a person to depression in adulthood. Research conclusion: hypothesis not supported in most depressives. Author biographical information. Abstract. 2 tables. Acknowledgement. 50 references.

1.437. Lloyd, Camille. "Life Events and Depressive Disorder Reviewed. II. Events as Precipitating Factors." **Archives of General Psychiatry** 37 (May 1980): 541-548.

Depressed persons, relative to normal controls or schizophrenics, experience more stressful events months preceding depression. Loss or severely threatening events are likely to precede depression. Although stressful events can precipitate depressive episodes, not all depressives report these events. Author biographical information. Abstract. 2 tables. Acknowledgement. 55 references.

1.438. Mayberry, Linda J. and Dyanne D. Affonso. "Infant Temperament and Postpartum Depression: A Review." **Health Care for Women International** 14 (March-April 1993): 201-211.

1.439. McKinney, William T., Jr. and William E. Bunney, Jr. "Animal Model of Depression. I. Review of Evidence: Implications for Research." **Archives of General Psychiatry** 21 (August 1969): 240-248.

The authors examine: (1) the need for an animal model of depression; (2) evidence for animal depression - for example, separation experiments, case histories; and (3) implications for research which includes, in part, induction of depression and minimal requirement for an animal model of depression. Author biographical information. 1 table. Acknowledgements. 45 references.

1.440. Minden, Sarah L. and Randolph B. Schiffer. "Affective Disorders in Multiple Sclerosis: Review and Recommendations for Clinical Research." **Archives of Neurology** 47 (January 1990): 98-104.

Information regarding euphoria; pathological laughing and weeping; depression; and bipolar affective disorder in multiple sclerosis (MS) was analyzed by members of the National Multiple Sclerosis Society Cognitive Function Study Group. Abstract. Author biographical information. 3 tables. Acknowledgements. 64 references.

1.441. Pfohl, Bruce, Ned Vasquez and Henry Nasrallah. "Unipolar vs. Bipolar Mania: A Review of 247 Patients." **British Journal of Psychiatry** 141 (November 1982): 453-458.

Data pertaining to 247 patients at the University of Iowa was analyzed. Each of these patients had had at least one manic episode. Eighty-seven of these patients had apparently never been depressed. A subgroup of ninety-two patients who had had at least two episodes of affective disorder were also studied. This review does not support the contention that unipolar mania is a separate entity from bipolar disorder. Abstract. 4 tables. 12 references. Author biographical information.

1.442. Richters, John E. "Depressed Mothers as Informants about Their Children: A Critical Review of the Evidence for Distortion." **Psychological Bulletin** 112 (November 1992): 485-499.

1.443. Silverman, Charlotte. "The Epidemiology of Depression - A Review." **American Journal of Psychiatry** 124 (January 1968): 883-891.

1.444. Stevens-Ratchford, Regena G. "The Effect of Life Review Reminiscence Activities on Depression and Self-Esteem in Older Adults." **American Journal of Occupational Therapy** 47 (May 1993): 413-420.

The subjects in this study were eight men and sixteen women, ranging in age from sixty-nine to ninety-one years. The subjects resided in a retirement community. They were assigned to experimental and comparison groups. The Beck Depression Inventory (BDI) and Rosenberg Self-Esteem Survey were used in this research. The research indicated that life review reminisence is a positive experience for older adults. Occupational therapists should consider incorporating life review reminiscence in programs for the elderly. Author biographical information. Abstract. 4 tables. Acknowledgements. 62 references.

1.445. Tisher, Miriam, Esther Lang-Takac and Moshe Lang. "The Children's Depression Scale: Review of Australian and Overseas Experience." **Australian Journal of Psychology** 44 (April 1992): 27-35.

1.446. Weinberg, Warren A. and Roger A. Brumback. "Mania in Childhood: Case Studies and Literature Review." **American Journal of Diseases of Children** 130 (April 1976): 380-385.

After an examination of five case studies, research results are reported in terms of: (1) criteria for diagnosis of mania in children versus adults; (2) criteria for diagnosis of depression in children versus adults; and (3) comparison of manic and depressive symptoms. Author biographical information. Abstract. 3 tables. 42 references. List of nonproprietary names and trademarks of drugs.

INFORMATION IN ENCYCLOPEDIAS

1.447. The Book of Health: A Medical Encyclopedia for Everyone, Third Edition, s.v. "Depressive Reaction."

1.448. The Canadian Medical Association Home Medical Encyclopedia, s.v. "Depression."

Depression experienced by some people, during most winters, is probably related to long hours of darkness during this time of year. At least 80% of suicides in Canada (about 14 per 100, 000) are related to depression. The suicide rate for natives in Canada is approximately 34 per 100,000. The rate for Indian males between twenty and twenty-four years of age is 170 per 100,000.

1.449. The Canadian Medical Association Home Medical Encyclopedia, s.v. "Melancholia."

1.450. Concise Encyclopedia of Psychology, s.v. "Antidepressive Drugs."

1.451. Concise Encyclopedia of Psychology, s.v. "Depression."

1.452. Concise Encyclopedia of Psychology, s.v. "Manic-Depressive Personality."

1.453. Encyclopedia of Clinical Assessment, s.v. "Depression."

Reference to depression and associated conditions have been made throughout history. Plutarch, in the second century, A.D., wrote about the helplessness of the depressed. The Greek physician Aretaeus of Cappadocia believed there was a relationship between melancholia and mania. Melancholia, in the Middle Ages, was thought of as a spell cast on a person by evil spirits. The French physician Philippe Pinel wrote, in the nineteenth century, about gloomy withdrawal in depressed patients. Emil Kraepelin made, circa 1896, a distinction between dementia praecox and manic-depressive psychosis, indicating that manic-depression is innate, and not caused by social and psychological forces. Adolf Meyer believed in 1908 that life's events do precipitate depression. 56 references.

1.454. The Encyclopedia of Human Behavior: Psychology, Psychiatry, and Mental Health, s.v. "Depression."

The death of a loved one or social rejection are overt situations associated with reactive depression. This depression tends to improve as the overt situation improves. A person, who is the object of an undesired obligation, may be the root cause of an endogenous depression. A mother, whose dependency on her daughter prevents the daughter from marrying, can be associated with endogenous depression. The daughter may unconsciously feel hostile toward the mother. The person who experiences endogenous depression is more likely to experience remorse, guilt, and sin than is the individual who experiences reactive depression. 1 illustrative case.

1.455. The Encyclopedia of Human Behavior: Psychology, Psychiatry, and Mental Health, s.v. "Melancholia."

1.456. The Encyclopedia of Human Behavior: Psychology, Psychiatry, and Mental Health, s.v. "Melancholic Personality."

Morose, sympathetic, overconscientious, perfectionistic, and indecisive are some of the words used to describe the melancholic personality. This type of person is always mildly depressed, cannot enjoy life, and is highly resistant to change.

1.457. The Encyclopedia of Medical Ignorance: Exploring the Frontiers of Medical Knowledge, s.v. "Depression."

When a person's behavior changes from normal behavior to a depressed state, the person experiences unipolar depression. When a person's behavior changes from normal behavior to a depressed state - and this state includes periods of mania - the person experiences bipolar depression. William James, Julian Huxley, Virginia Woolf, Ernest Hemingway, and Albert Einstein are examples of eminent people who experienced depression. Author biographical information. 2 photographs. 6 figures. 12 references.

1.458. International Encyclopedia of Psychiatry, Psychology, Psychoanalysis, and Neurology, s.v. "Affective Disorders: Genetics."

1.459. International Encyclopedia of Psychiatry, Psychology, Psychoanalysis, and Neurology, s.v. "Depression and Mania: Psychoanalytic Theories."

1.460. International Encyclopedia of Psychiatry, Psychology, Psychoanalysis, and Neurology, s.v. "Depression: Horney's View."

1.461. International Encyclopedia of Psychiatry, Psychology, Psychoanalysis, and Neurology, s.v. "Depression: Pharmacologic Treatment."

1.462. International Encyclopedia of Psychiatry, Psychology, Psychoanalysis, and Neurology, s.v. "Depression: Psychotherapy."

INFORMATION IN BOOKS OF QUOTATIONS

1.463. The Beacon Book of Quotations by Women, s.v. "Depression."

Comments by May Sarton, Stevie Smith, Lisa Alther, Kate Millett, Carol Bly, Nadine Gordimer, Patricia Moyes, Erma Bombeck, and Dodie Smith.

1.464. The Columbia Dictionary of Quotations, s.v. "Depression."

Quotations by Jean Baudrillard, Leonard Cohen, Judith Guest, Ernest Hemingway, Eric Hoffer, William James, John Keats, Soren Kierkegaard, and Susan Sontag.

1.465. The Crown Treasury of Relevant Quotations, s.v. "Depression."

Wilhelm Stekel, Nathaniel Hawthorne, D.H. Lawrence, Jeromek Jerome, and May Sarton are quoted.

1.466. The Home Book of Quotations: Classical and Modern, Tenth Edition, s.v. "Melancholy."

Some of the individuals whose quotations are listed are Aristotle, Thomas Browne, Robert Burton, Samuel Johnson, Susannah Centlivre, William Collins, John Dyer, John Fletcher, John Ford, Thomas Gray, Thomas Hood, Victor Hugo, Samuel Rogers, H.K. White, Ben Jonson, W.M. Praed, and Aphra Behn.

1.467. The Macmillan Dictionary of Quotations, s.v. "Melancholy."

Comments by Francis Beaumont, Robert Burton, T.S. Eliot, John Keats, Martin Luther, John Milton, and Stephen Vizinczey.

1.468. The New Dictionary of Thoughts: A Cyclopedia of Quotations, Revised Edition, s.v. "Melancholy."

A few of the persons quoted include John Gibson Lockhart, Lydia M. Child, P.B. Power, Sydney Smith, Margaret Fuller, and Jonathan Edwards.

VIDEOCASSETTES

1.469. The Depressed Client. 30 minutes. 1977. Distributed/Produced by American Journal of Nursing Company, New York, NY.

1.470. The Depressed Patient. 2.5 hours. 1980. Distributed/Produced by American Medical Association, Chicago, IL.

1.471. The Depressed Patient: Nursing in the Acute Care Setting. 28 minutes. 1989. Distributed/Produced by American Journal of Nursing Company, New York, NY.

1.472. **Depression.** 28 minutes. 1984. Distributed/Produced by Filmakers Library, Inc., New York, NY.

1.473. **Depression and Suicide.** 26 minutes. 1976. Distributed/Produced by Cinema Guild, New York, NY.

1.474. **Depression: Beyond the Darkness.** 50 minutes. 1990. Distributed/Produced by MPI Home Video, Oak Forest, IL.

1.475. **Depression: Biology of the Blues.** 26 minutes. 1988. Distributed/Produced by Films for the Humanities, Princeton, NJ.

1.476. **Depression: Blahs, Blues, and Better Days.** 18 minutes. 1973. Distributed/Produced by AEF/Capital Communications, Nashville, TN.

1.477. **Depression: The Dark Side of the Blues.** 25 minutes. 1987. Distributed/Produced by Barr Films, Irwindale, CA.

1.478. **Depression in Cancer Patients: A Neuropsychiatric Approach.** 60 minutes. 1981. Distributed/Produced by University of Texas M.D. Anderson Cancer Center, Houston, TX.

1.479. **Depression...More Than Just the Blues.** 28 minutes. 1988. Distributed/Produced by Milner-Fenwick, Inc., Timonium, MD.

1.480. **Depression: Signs and Symptoms.** 10 minutes. 1988. Distributed/Produced by Professional Research, Inc., Evanston, IL.

1.481. **Depression/Stress.** 20 minutes. 1989. Distributed/Produced by United Learning, Inc., Niles, IL.

1.482. **Depression: A Study in Abnormal Behavior.** 27 minutes. 1973. Distributed/Produced by CRM/McGraw Hill Films, Del Mar, CA.

1.483. **Depression: Use and Side Effects of Medication.** 10 minutes. 1988. Distributed/Produced by Professional Research, Inc., Evanston, IL.

Chapter 2

CASE EXAMPLES

BOOKS FOR PROFESSIONALS AND THE GENERAL PUBLIC

2.001. Blackburn, Ivy-Marie and Kate M. Davidson. **Cognitive Therapy for Depression and Anxiety: A Practitioner's Guide.** Oxford: Blackwell Scientific, 1990.

A generation ago psychoanalysis and its derivatives and the behavior therapy of B.F. Skinner and H. Eysenck dominated thinking and practice. Twenty-five years later, A.T. Beck's cognitive therapy has come into favor. This therapy's techniques are, unlike those of psychoanalysis and behavior therapy, easily described, human in its origins/applications, and rationale based on reasoned arguments. Furthermore, the same cognitive therapy techniques are often used to treat different disorders.

2.002. Hirschfeld, Robert M.A. and Susan Meltsner. **When the Blues Won't Go Away: New Approaches to Dysthymic Disorder and Other Forms of Chronic Low-Grade Depression.** New York, NY: Macmillan, 1991.

Dysthymic disorder (DD) is a low-grade depression. It arises during a life trauma and can persist for years. DD is sometimes misdiagnosed. Other times the person who has DD believes it is only "the Blues." There may be more than 5 million Americans who have DD.

2.003. Schad-Somers, Susanne P. **On Mood Swings: The Psychobiology of Elation and Depression.** New York, NY: Plenum, 1990.

CHAPTERS AND SECTIONS IN BOOKS FOR PROFESSIONALS AND THE GENERAL PUBLIC

2.004. Alexander, Matthew. "Anxiety and Depression." Chapter in **Essentials of Family Medicine,** edited by Philip D. Sloane, Lisa M. Slatt and Richard M. Baker, 209-216. Baltimore, MD: Williams and Wilkins, 1988.

Many people who visit their family physician are depressed, but are not aware depression is their problem. These individuals may complain about headache, fatigue, or memory loss. Their condition is masked depression. Severe depression is associated with approximately 80% of suicides. Between 5% and 15% of severely depressed persons commit suicide. 3 tables. 5 references.

2.005. Baker, Howard S. "Case Example." in **Handbook of Short-Term Dynamic Psychotherapy,** edited by Paul Crits-Christoph and Jacques P. Barber, 312-317. N.p., BasicBooks, 1991.

2.006. Baron, Robert A., Donn Byrne and Barry H. Kantowitz. "Case History: Reactive Depression: Giving Up in Despair." in **Psychology: Understanding Behavior,** Second Edition, by Robert A. Baron, Donn Byrne and Barry H. Kantowitz, 539-542. New York, NY: Holt, Rinehart and Winston, 1980.

2.007. Bedi, Ashok R. "Affective Disorders." in **Alcohol and Drug Abuse Handbook,** edited by Roland E. Herrington, George R. Jacobson and David G. Benzer, 363-367. St. Louis, MO: Warren H. Green, 1987.

The Dexamethasone Suppression Test (DMST) can be used to diagnose depression. This test is a blood test which is relatively inexpensive and can be administered to outpatients. However, marijuana use and hepatic disease can invalidate test results.

2.008. Bedi, Ashok R. "Dysthymic Disorder." in **Alcohol and Drug Abuse Handbook,** edited by Roland E. Herrington, George R. Jacobson and David G. Benzer, 360-362. St. Louis, MO: Warren H. Green, 1987.

A person who has a dysthymic disorder in early adolescence, or earlier, may have the basis for alcoholism, or other substance abuse disorder, later in life. If one of these disorders becomes evident, the disorder serves to mask depressed mood and low self-esteem. It is important to consider four aspects of treatment, including the fact that, for this group, antidepressant medication is generally not beneficial.

2.009. Bedrosian, Richard C. "Treating Depression and Suicidal Wishes within the Family Context." Chapter in **Cognitive-Behavioral Therapy with Families,** edited by Norman Epstein, Stephen E. Schlesinger and Windy Dryden, 292-324. New York, NY: Brunner/Mazel, 1988.

2.010. Beier, Ernst G. and Evans G. Valens. "Depression and Suicide as Communication." Chapter in **People-Reading: How We Control Others, How They Control Us,** by Ernst G. Beier and Evans G. Valens, 165-177. New York, NY: Stein and Day, 1975.

Although depression is related to sulking, depression involves real suffering. A loss - even loss of a skill - can cause depression. Depression seems to be an attempt to punish someone else by self-hurting. The depressed person is not aware of the aggressive component in depression.

2.011. Beitman, Bernard D. "Systematic Technical Eclecticism: Two Depressive Episodes Treated with Very Brief Psychotherapy." Chapter in **Casebook of Eclectic Psychotherapy,** edited by John C. Norcross, 19-47. New York, NY: Brunner/Mazel, 1987.

2.012. Beres, David. "Superego and Depression." in **Psychoanalysis - A General Psychology: Essays in Honor of Heinz Hartmann,** edited by Rudolph M. Loewenstein, Lottie M. Newman, Max Schur and Albert J. Solnit, 479-498. New York, NY: International Universities Press, 1966.

2.013. Bernard, Michael E. and Marie R. Joyce. "Depression." in **Rational-Emotive Therapy with Children and Adolescents: Theory, Treatment Strategies, Preventative Methods,** by Michael E. Bernard and Marie R. Joyce, 310-311. New York, NY: John Wiley and Sons, 1984.

Penny was a fourteen-year-old schoolgirl who had a hearing loss, a perfectionistic father, and four older brothers. She not only felt inadequate when compared to her brothers, she felt nervous and lonely when she was not with them. Rational-emotive therapy helped her challenge her irrational beliefs about herself. She attended eight sessions before she felt better. She began doing her schoolwork without comparing herself to other indiviudals.

2.014. Biglan, Anthony and David R. Campbell. "Depression." Chapter in **Behavioral Assignments and Treatment Compliance: A Handbook of Clinical Strategies,** by John L. Shelton and Rona L. Levy, 111-146. Champaign, IL: Research Press, 1981.

2.015. Bird, Brian. "The Depressed Patient and the Suicidal Patient." Chapter in **Talking with Patients,** Second Edition, by Brian Bird, 139-164. Philadelphia, PA: J.B. Lippincott Company, 1973.

2.016. Bloomfield, Harold H. "Depression." in **Modern Therapies,** edited by Virginia Binder, Arnold Binder and Bernard Rimland, 106-108. Englewood Cliffs, NJ: Prentice-Hall, 1976.

The patient was a twenty-six-year-old female with a long history of depression and suicide attempts. She was a teacher troubled by student and family problems. After six months in a TM (Transcendental Meditation) program, she stated the program calmed her down and gave her more energy. She had not responded very well in the past to psychiatry. TM apparently releases daily stresses, gradually resolves older conflicts, and counteracts chronic anxiety, eliminating stress and fatigue. 1 figure.

2.017. Brill, Leon. "Case 3, Debra Scott: Depression as a Central Feature in Treatment." in **The Clinical Treatment of Substance Abusers,** by Leon Brill, 89-91. New York, NY: Free Press, 1981.

Debra Scott, a white female, began using heroin at age twenty-six. She was married by age thirty and participating in a methadone maintenance program. She had been abusing amphetamines prior to receiving methadone treatment.

2.018. Butler, Pamela. "Depression." in **Self-Assertion for Women,** New Edition, by Pamela Butler, 27-28. San Francisco, CA: Harper and Row, 1981.

The traditional feminine role, compared to the traditional masculine role, has been characterized in terms of helplessness, lack of reinforcement, and nonrecognition. This may help explain why twice as many women as men experience depression.

2.019. Butler, Pamela. "Depression: The Lack of Positive Reinforcement." in **Self-Assertion for Women,** New Edition, by Pamela Butler, 31-32. San Francisco, CA: Harper and Row, 1981.

Men have more external rewards than women. This disparity can be attributed to the feminine role - marriage, home, children. Depression accompanies the empty nest syndrome as does a lack of positive reinforcement, when women experience this condition. Women who work often have lower status and are in poorly paid positions.

2.020. Campbell, Thomas and Susan McDaniel. "Depression." in **The Family in Medical Practice: A Family Systems Primer,** edited by Michael A. Crouch and Leonard Roberts, 130-133. New York, NY: Springer Verlag, 1987.

The biomedical explanation for depression attributes depression to imbalances of norepinephrine and serotonin in the brain. Tricyclic antidepressants and monoamine oxidase inhibitors are recommended medication for depression. The psychodynamic explanation of depression contends depression arises from intrapsychic conflicts associated with early childhood experiences. It is claimed that years of psychotherapy are necessary to resolve the conflicts. A systems approach does not only incorporate the biomedical and psychodynamic explanations, but also includes the family, and other individuals involved in interpersonal events.

2.021. Carlton, Peter L. "Lithium and the Antidepressants." Chapter in **A Primer of Behavioral Pharmacology: Concepts and Principles in the Behavioral Analysis of Drug Action,** by Peter L. Carlton, 211-232. New York, NY: W.H. Freeman and Company, 1983.

2.022. Charatan, Fred B., Fredrick T. Sherman and Leslie S. Libow. "Depression in Old Age." in **The Core of Geriatric Medicine: A Guide for Students and Practitioners,** 70-75. St. Louis, MO: C.V. Mosby, 1981.

Loss of physical vigor, memory, hearing, hair, and status are some of the reasons for depression in old age. The primary care physician should be aware of illnesses that imitate depression. Hypothyroidism, apathetic hyperthyroidism, cerebral neoplasm, and parkinsonism are some of these illnesses. 1 figure. 1 table.

2.023. Chess, Stella and Mahin Hassibi. "Depression." in **Principles and Practice of Child Psychiatry,** Second Edition, by Stella Chess and Mahin Hassibi, 145-149. New York, NY: Plenum, 1986.

2.024. Christie-Seely, Janet, Gilles Paradis and Renée Turcotte. "Case 5: The Origins and Maintenance of Depression." in **Working with the Family in Primary Care: A Systems Approach to Health and Illness**, edited by Janet Christie-Seely, 303-307. New York, NY: Praeger, 1984.

2.025. Coates, Dan and Camille B. Wortman. "Depression Maintenance and Interpersonal Control." Chapter in **Advances in Environmental Psychology, Volume 2: Applications of Personal Control**, edited by Andrew Baum and Jerome E. Singer, 149-182. Hillsdale, NJ: Lawrence Erlbaum Associates, 1980.

2.026. Cohen, Susan and Daniel Cohen. "Depression." in **Teenage Stress,** by Susan Cohen and Daniel Cohen, 128-133. New York, NY: M. Evans and Company, 1984.

How people feel, not how they act, is the more accurate indicator of depression. Depressed teenagers do not necessarily move slowly, sleep a lot, or cry. Teenagers, because they have considerable energy, can be very depressed, at the same time they exhibit hyper behavior.

2.027. Custer, Robert and Harry Milt. "Relief from Anxiety and Depression." in **When Luck Runs Out: Help for Compulsive Gamblers and Their Families,** by Robert Custer and Harry Milt, 124-125. New York, NY: Warner Books, 1985.

Compulsive gamblers need relief from anxiety and tension. Some compulsive gamblers are addicted to gambling and alcohol, others to gambling, alcohol, and drugs. Double and triple addictions, however, are rare for these individuals. There does not appear to be a scientific answer for this.

2.028. Danielson, Carol B., Brenda Hamel-Bissell and Patricia Winstead-Fry. "Acute, Recurrent, and Resolvable Mental Illness: Depression." Chapter in **Families, Health and Illness: Perspectives on Coping and Intervention,** by Carol B. Danielson, Brenda Hamel-Bissell and Patricia Winstead-Fry, 377-403. St. Louis, MO: Mosby Year Book, 1993.

The Resiliency Model of Family Stress, Adjustment, and Adaptation is used to illustrate family coping with depression. The model is applied to the: (1) family situation; (2) illness: depression; (3) demands of the illness stressor; (4) resources available to the family; (5) family appraisals of the illness situation, and (6) family interventions. This model is based on the work of Drs. Marilyn A. McCubbin and Hamilton I. McCubbin of the University of Wisconsin. 3 figures. 27 references.

2.029. Davis, Glenn C. and Beth Goldman. "Pharmacotherapy of Depression." in **Review of General Psychiatry,** Third Edition, edited by Howard H. Goldman, 371-376. Norwalk, CT: Appleton and Lange, 1992.

Dry mouth, constipation, tremor, palpitation, and weight gain are some of the adverse effects of antidepressants. 2 tables.

2.030. Davis, Glenn C. and Beth Goldman. "Pharmacotherapy of Mania." in **Review of General Psychiatry,** Third Edition, edited by Howard H. Goldman, 376-378. Norwalk, CT: Appleton and Lange, 1992.

Carbamazepine and valproic acid - both are anticonvulsants - and lithium are used to treat manic episodes. Lithium, when used to treat acute mania, is over 95% effective. Thirst, tremor, and vomiting are a few of the negative effects of lithium.

2.031. De Rosis, Helen A. "Anxiety and Depression." in **Women and Anxiety: A Step-by-Step Program for Managing Anxiety and Depression,** by Helen A. De Rosis, 116-119. New York, NY: Delacorte, 1979.

Feelings of inferiority, loss, poor self-esteem, and apprehensiveness are some of the feelings common to both anxious and depressed persons. Inherent restlessness is associated with anxious states. Inactivity and a basic hopelessness is associated with depression. An agitated depression results when anxiety and depression appear in the same person. The depression results when individuals, who are hypersensitive to conflict and anxiety, unconsciously choose to be depressed, rather than anxious. Depression in such situations is more bearable.

2.032. De Rosis, Helen A. "Covert Depression." in **Women and Anxiety: A Step-by-Step Program for Managing Anxiety and Depression,** by Helen A. De Rosis, 251-252. New York, NY: Delacorte, 1979.

2.033. Diamond, John. "Depression." in **Life Energy: Understanding and Transforming Your Emotions to Achieve Total Health,** by John Diamond, 165-171. New York, NY: Dodd, Mead and Company, 1985.

There is evidence of hypothyroidism in at least 70% of the patients Dr. John Diamond sees in his practice. Most people who have hypothyroidism state they are most tired in the morning. Loss of hair and baldness, as well as depression, is commonly noted in this condition. 1 photograph.

2.034. Dorcus, Roy M. and G. Wilson Shaffer. "Depressed States." in **Textbook of Abnormal Psychology,** Third Edition, by Roy M. Dorcus and G. Wilson Shaffer, 344-351. Baltimore, MD: Williams and Wilkins, 1945.

2.035. Dorcus, Roy M. and G. Wilson Shaffer. "Involutional Melancholia." in **Textbook of Abnormal Psychology,** Third Edition, by Roy M. Dorcus and G. Wilson Shaffer, 351-353. Baltimore, MD: Williams and Wilkins, 1945.

The involutional period occurs in women when they are between forty and fifty-five years of age and in men when they are between fifty and sixty-five. There is a gradual decline in health, increase in chronic illness, and realization that new ventures will not likely be undertaken. There may be feelings of unreality, hypochondriacal delusions, preoccupation with death, insomnia, anxiety, and depression. The basis of involutional melancholia may be decreased sex hormone production.

2.036. Earle, Ralph and Gregory Crow. "Depression." in **Lonely All the Time: Recognizing, Understanding and Overcoming Sex Addiction, for Addicts and Co-Dependents**, by Ralph Earle and Gregory Crow, 184-186. New York, NY: Pocket Books, 1989.

Men and women, whether in a marital or nonmarital relationship, cannot single-handedly cure the sex addiction of their partner. The nonaddict in the relationship experiences guilt and depression, when the partner cannot be reformed and the relationship improved. The nonaddicted partner begins his own recovery from guilt and depression, when he realizes his powerlessness to change the addict.

2.037. Earle, Ralph and Gregory Crow. "Depression." in **Lonely All the Time: Recognizing, Understanding and Overcoming Sex Addiction, for Addicts and Co-Dependents**, by Ralph Earle and Gregory Crow, 280. New York, NY: Pocket Books, 1989.

Anger turned inward, negative self-talk, and self-criticism are sources of depression. Persons who increase their personal power realize they do not have to feel responsible - guilty and depressed - because their sexual partner is addicted to sex.

2.038. Fanning, Patrick. "Depression, Anxiety, and Anger." Chapter in **Visualization for Change: A Step-by-Step Guide to Using Your Powers of Imagination for Self-Improvement, Therapy, Healing, and Pain Control**, by Patrick Fanning, 171-193. Oakland, CA: New Harbinger Publications, 1988.

2.039. Fensterheim, Herbert and Jean Baer. "Lack of Reinforcers = Depression." Chapter in **Don't Say Yes When You Want to Say No: How Assertiveness Training Can Change Your Life**, by Herbert Fensterheim and Jean Baer, 176-181. New York, NY: David McKay, 1975.

Laboratory exercises can provide positive reinforcement, via fantasy, to help relieve depression, and can also generate plans to help find new sources for positive reinforcement. Chronic depression results from a lack of positive reinforcers.

2.040. Freudenberger, Herbert J. and Gail North. "Depression." in **Women's Burnout: How to Spot It, How to Reverse It, and How to Prevent It**, by Herbert J. Freudenberger and Gail North, 109-112. Garden City, NY: Doubleday and Company, 1985. Reprint. Harmondsworth, England: Penguin, 1986.

Depression is the eleventh stage of the twelve-stage Burnout Symptom Cycle. This stage is extremely serious because it precedes the last stage, Total Burnout Exhaustion. Life at the eleventh stage seems hopeless, despair is prevalent, and there is desire for continual sleep. There is virtually no self-esteem, but there are suicidal ideas. Professional help must be sought.

2.041. Gaev, Dorothy Meyer. "Depression." in **The Psychology of Loneliness**, by Dorothy Meyer Gaev, 88-92. Chicago, IL: Adams, 1976.

There are various sources of emotional nourishment. Another person is perhaps the most common source. There are also nonhuman sources. Music and books are examples. Depressed persons should not be overly dependent on other people for emotional needs, and should also rely on nonhuman sources.

2.042. Galanter, Marc. "Secondary Depression." in **Network Therapy for Alcohol and Drug Abuse: A New Approach in Practice**, by Marc Galanter, 62-65. New York, NY: Basic Books, 1993.

Depressed mood is common in detoxifying substance abusers, including alcoholics and cocaine abusers. Suicidal ideation is also common in both types of abusers. The treatment of a forty-year-old actor, who abused alcohol and cocaine, illustrates the use of a combined treatment approach.

2.043. Glass, Ilana Belle and Jane Marshall. "Depressive Illness." in **The International Handbook of Addiction Behaviour**, edited by Ilana Belle Glass, 157-158. London: Routledge, 1991.

Antidepressants were effective in the treatment of two alcoholics, a married woman, late thirties, and a married man, late forties. The woman drank to relieve depression, but had become more depressed. The man had been a heavy drinker for twenty years. He had remained abstinent for a year after treatment, but had resumed drinking after the death of his father.

2.044. Glass, Ilana Belle and Jane Marshall. "Hypomania." in **The International Handbook of Addiction Behaviour**, edited by Ilana Belle Glass, 158. London: Routledge, 1991.

A single professional woman in her mid-thirties - afflicted with bipolar affective disorder and alcohol dependence - was hospitalized and treated with neuroleptics, after becoming very active, talking in a loud voice, relapsing into heavy drinking, and seeing visions of Jesus.

2.045. Glick, Ira D. "Case 6." in **The Impaired Physician**, edited by Stephen C. Scheiber and Brian B. Doyle, 104-105. New York, NY: Plenum, 1983.

Depression in a couple in their forties - the husband a physician - who underwent marital therapy and were prescribed antidepressant medication.

2.046. Golomb, Sylvia L. and Andrea Kocsis. "Bipolar Illness." in **The Halfway House: On the Road to Independence**, by Sylvia L. Golomb and Andrea Kocsis, 26-27. New York, NY: Brunner/Mazel, 1988.

2.047. Golomb, Sylvia L. and Andrea Kocsis. "Depression." in **The Halfway House: On the Road to Independence**, by Sylvia L. Golomb and Andrea Kocsis, 25-26. New York, NY: Brunner/Mazel, 1988.

2.048. Greenwald, Harold. "Depression." in **The Call Girl: A Social and Psychoanalytic Study**, by Harold Greenwald, 139. New York, NY: Ballantine Books, 1958.

Dr. Harold Greenwald, a graduate of Columbia University and Executive Director of the Association for Applied Psychoanalysis, incorporated six years of research with knowledge gained during his clinical treatment of call girls, to form the basis of this book.

2.049. Gruetzner, Howard. "Depression and Alzheimer's." Chapter in **Alzheimer's A Caregiver's Guide and Sourcebook**, Updated and Revised, by Howard Gruetzner, 37-44. New York, NY: John Wiley and Sons, 1992.

2.050. Halpern, Howard M. "Anxiety vs. Depression." in **How to Break Your Addiction to a Person**, by Howard M. Halpern, 77-82. New York, NY: Bantam Books, 1982.

2.051. Halpern, Howard M. "Joy vs. Depression." in **How to Break Your Addiction to a Person,** by Howard M. Halpern, 76-77. New York, NY: Bantam Books, 1982.

2.052. Herskowitz, Joel and N. Paul Rosman. "Depression." Chapter in **Pediatrics, Neurology, and Psychiatry - Common Ground; Behavioral, Cognitive, Affective, and Physical Disorders in Childhood and Adolescence,** by Joel Herskowitz and N. Paul Rosman, 111-138. New York, NY: Macmillan, 1982.

Some causes of depression: (1) medical (hypothyroidism); (2) neurologic (migraine); (3) toxic (alcohol); (4) psychologic (reaction to change); (5) social-environmental (situational events); (6) genetic-constitutional (bipolar affective disorder); and (7) developmental (age-related stresses). 5 tables. 5 figures. 54 references.

2.053. Hindy, Carl G., J. Conrad Schwarz and Archie Brodsky. "Depression: Love's Hangover." Chapter in **If This Is Love, Why Do I Feel So Insecure?,** by Carl G. Hindy, J. Conrad Schwarz and Archie Brodsky, 200-230. New York, NY: Atlantic Monthly Press, 1989.

2.054. Hodgson, Ray and Peter Miller. "Lifting Depression." Chapter in **Selfwatching: Addictions, Habits, Compulsions: What to Do about Them,** by Ray Hodgson and Peter Miller, 67-79. New York, NY: Facts on File, 1982.

Problem drinking, overeating, and compulsive hand-washing are a few activities associated with depression. Depression makes it very difficult to initiate activity and very difficult to resist compulsive urges. The psychological approach of Aaron Beck can be used to treat depression. 14 photographs.

2.055. Hollingsworth, Charles E. "Case 4: Cystic Fibrosis with Depression." in **Pediatric Consultation Liaison Psychiatry,** edited by Charles E. Hollingsworth, 89-90. New York, NY: SP Medical and Scientific Books, 1983.

Jackie, a fourteen-year-old female, diagnosed with cystic fibrosis, felt she could not trust anyone - parents nor medical staff - after no one, initially, would tell her truthfully about her medical condition.

2.056. Hollingsworth, Charles E. "Case 11: Seizure Disorder, Depression, Behavior Problem." in **Pediatric Consultation Liaison Psychiatry,** edited by Charles E. Hollingsworth, 101-104. New York, NY: SP Medical and Scientific Books, 1983.

2.057. Hollingsworth, Charles E. "Case 13: Transverse Myelitis and Depression." in **Pediatric Consultation Liaison Psychiatry,** edited by Charles E. Hollingsworth, 106-109. New York, NY: SP Medical and Scientific Books, 1983.

A thirteen-year-old male has reactive depression which is secondary to acute illness.

2.058. Hollingsworth, Charles E. "Case 20: Chronic Immunodeficiency Disease with Depression." in **Pediatric Consultation Liaison Psychiatry,** edited by Charles E. Hollingsworth, 123-126. New York, NY: SP Medical and Scientific Books, 1983.

2.059. Hooker, Carol E. "Loss and Depression." in **Social Work Processes,** Third Edition, by Beulah Roberts Compton and Burt Galaway, 52-53. Homewood, IL: Dorsey, 1984.

2.060. Horowitz, Mardi J. "Example of Depression after the Death of a Loved One." in **Handbook of Short-Term Dynamic Psychotherapy,** edited by Paul Crits-Christoph and Jacques P. Barber, 187-188. N.p., BasicBooks, 1991.

2.061. Hutt, Max L. and Robert Gwyn Gibby. "Depressive and Manic Psychoses." in **Patterns of Abnormal Behavior,** by Max L. Hutt and Robert Gwyn Gibby, 290-304. Boston, MA: Allyn and Bacon, 1957.

Emil Kraepelin in 1904 classified and described the manic and depressive syndrome. Symptoms, however, were noted as early as 1025 B.C. Beethoven, Tolstoy, and Dickens are a few great men who had manic-depressive psychoses. Forrestal, the first U.S. Secretary of Defense, probably had a manic-depressive personality. The person who has involutional melancholia is likely to live in a rural area, is likely to be married, and, in the U.S., is likely to be white. The manic individual has incoherent speech and uses disjointed phrases. The manic, unlike the schizophrenic, is in touch with reality. 1 table. 1 figure.

2.062. Izard, Carroll E. "Sadness in Grief and Depression." Chapter in **The Psychology of Emotions**, by Carroll E. Izard, 203-227. New York, NY: Plenum, 1991.

2.063. Jacobson, Edith. "Problems in the Differentiation between Schizophrenic and Melancholic States of Depression." in **Psychoanalysis - A General Psychology: Essays in Honor of Heinz Hartmann**, edited by Rudolph M. Loewenstein, Lottie M.

Newman, Max Schur and Albert J. Solnit, 499-518. New York, NY: International Universities Press, 1966.

2.064. Jacobson, Neil S. and Gayla Margolin. "Depression." in **Marital Therapy: Strategies Based on Social Learning and Behavior Exchange Principles,** by Neil S. Jacobson and Gayla Margolin, 305-312. New York, NY: Brunner/Mazel, 1979.

The recommended therapy for depression in marriage is conjoint therapy, when the relationship, rather than extrarelationship variables, is the source of depression.

2.065. Janda, Louis H. and Karin E. Klenke-Hamel. "The Affective Psychoses." in **Psychology: Its Study and Uses,** by Louis H. Janda and Karin E. Klenke-Hamel, 354-358. New York, NY: St. Martin's Press, 1982.

2.066. Janov, Arthur. "Depression." in **The Primal Scream,** by Arthur Janov, 72-74. New York, NY: Dell, 1970.

2.067. Janowsky, David S., Dominick Addario and Marc A. Schuckit. "Case 15: Treatment of Unipolar Depression." in **Psychopharmacology Case Studies: A Compilation of 53 Case Histories,** by David S. Janowsky, Dominick Addario and Marc A. Schuckit, 53-55. Garden City, NY: Medical Examination Publishing, 1978.

2.068. Janowsky, David S., Dominick Addario and Marc A. Schuckit. "Case 24: Treatment of Depression in the Elderly." in **Psychopharmacology Case Studies: A Compilation of 53 Case Histories,** by David S. Janowsky, Dominick Addario and Marc A. Schuckit, 79-82. Garden City, NY: Medical Examination Publishing, 1978.

2.069. Janowsky, David S., Dominick Addario and Marc A. Schuckit. "Case 25: Utilization of Antidepressants in the Elderly." in **Psychopharmacology Case Studies: A Compilation of 53 Case Histories,** by David S. Janowsky, Dominick Addario and Marc A. Schuckit, 82-83. Garden City, NY: Medical Examination Publishing, 1978.

2.070. Janowsky, David S., Dominick Addario and Marc A. Schuckit. "Case 51: Depression Associated with Oral Contraceptives." in **Psychopharmacology Case Studies: A Compilation of 53 Case Histories,** by David S. Janowsky, Dominick Addario and Marc A. Schuckit, 169-171. Garden City, NY: Medical Examination Publishing, 1978.

2.071. Jelliffe, Smith Ely and William A. White. "Manic-Depressive Psychoses." Chapter in **An Outline of Abnormal Psychology,** edited by Gardner Murphy, 113-128. New York, NY: Modern Library, 1929.

2.072. Johnson, Karen and Tom Ferguson. "Depression." Chapter in **Trusting Ourselves: The Sourcebook on Psychology for Women,** by Karen Johnson and Tom Ferguson, 241-270. New York, NY: Atlantic Monthly Press, 1990.

2.073. Johnson, Sherry E. "Depression." in **After a Child Dies: Counseling Bereaved Families,** by Sherry E. Johnson, 86-88. New York, NY: Springer, 1987.

Grief depression is experienced by a person who grieves after the death of a child. The symptoms of this depression should, several months after the death of the child, decrease or fluctuate. There is probably a clinical depression if, after several months, symptoms have increased significantly.

2.074. Kaplan, Harold I. and Benjamin J. Sadock. "Mood Disorders." Chapter in **Synopsis of Psychiatry: Behavioral Sciences, Clinical Psychiatry,** Fifth Edition, by Harold I. Kaplan and Benjamin J. Sadock, 288-309. Baltimore, MD: Williams and Wilkins, 1988.

Analysis of the epidemiology; etiology; clinical signs and symptoms; course and prognosis; and other aspects of mood disorders is essential to the understanding of these conditions. Depressive and bipolar disorders and dysthymia and cyclothymia are examples of mood disorders. 1 figure. 19 tables. 20 references.

2.075. Kaufman, Gershen. "Developing Equal Power: A Case Involving a Depressive Syndrome." in **The Psychology of Shame: Theory and Treatment of Shame-Based Syndromes,** by Gershen Kaufman, 239-244. New York, NY: Springer, 1989.

Emily was a middle-aged, divorced single parent, who lived with her two sons. She sought help because of acute depression. A year and a half prior to seeking help she had been subjected to a number of stressors, including major surgery, the death of a brother in a freak accident, and her father's heart attack. She overcame her depression through therapy, learning how to develop equal power in family interaction, and how to preserve her dignity.

2.076. Kendler, Howard H. "Manic-Depressive Psychosis." in **Basic Psychology,** Third Edition, by Howard H. Kendler, 608-611. Menlo Park, CA: W.A. Benjamin, 1974.

2.077. Koenig, Harold G. and Dan G. Blazer, II. "Depression and Other Affective Disorders." Chapter in **Geriatric Medicine,** Second Edition, edited by Christine K. Cassel, Donald E. Riesenberg, Leif B. Sorensen and John R. Walsh, 473-490. New York, NY: Springer-Verlag, 1990.

2.078. Krupski, Ann Marie. "Depression." in **Inside the Adolescent Alcoholic**, by Ann Marie Krupski, 21-27. N.p., Hazelden, 1982.

2.079. Kuperman, Samuel and Mark A. Stewart. "Grief and Depression." Chapter in **Behavioral Problems in Childhood: A Primary Care Approach**, edited by Stewart Gabel, 393-398. New York, NY: Grune and Stratton, 1981.

Depression can be diagnosed with the aid of the **Diagnostic and Statistical Manual of Mental Disorders** of the American Psychiatric Association. Psychoanalytic theory views depression as usually resulting from a loss - an important individual during childhood - and subsequent memories of the loss, accompanied by anger turned inward. Behaviorists believe depression is caused by insufficient positive reinforcement. Cognitive therapists contend that negative cognitions explain depression. The medical model assumes depression consists of different variables which comprise a psychiatric syndrome. Dry mouth, constipation, and tachycardia are some of the side effects when imipramine is used to treat depression. Electroconvulsive therapy (ECT) can save the life of a depressed adolescent if, for example, this adolescent refuses to eat or is suicidal. 1 table. 10 references.

2.080. LeMaistre, JoAnn. "Intermittent Depression." Chapter in **Beyond Rage: Mastering Unavoidable Health Changes,** Revised and Expanded Edition, by JoAnn LeMaistre, 116-131. Oak Park, IL: Alpine Guild, 1993.

A middle-aged, male stroke victim is profiled.

2.081. Lerner, Harriet Goldhor. "So, Who's Responsible for Claire's Depression?" in **The Dance of Intimacy: A Woman's Guide to Courageous Acts of Change in Key Relationships,** by Harriet Goldhor Lerner, 180-182. New York, NY: Harper and Row, 1989.

2.082. Lever, Judy and Michael G. Brush. "Coping with Your Moods." Chapter in **Premenstrual Tension,** by Judy Lever and Michael G. Brush, 95-101. New York, NY: McGraw-Hill, 1981.

Female tissues can retain water and alcohol during the premenstrual week, except that alcohol is absorbed more quickly. The PMT (premenstrual tension) sufferer who consumes alcohol at this time can easily become intoxicated. To drink to temporarily relieve anxiety and depression can lead to a monthly routine of alcohol abuse. In Britain the largest alcoholism clinic, ACCEPT, helps women keep informed about the pressures of PMT.

2.083. M., Earle. "Discontent, Depression, and Acceptance." in **Physician, Heal Thyself!,** by Earle M., 90-91. Minneapolis, MN: Compcare, 1989.

2.084. Madanes, Cloe. "Case 1: A Depressed Man." in **Strategic Family Therapy,** by Cloe Madanes, 34-39. San Francisco, CA: Jossey-Bass, 1984.

The details of this case are presented on pages 178-215 of the above book.

2.085. Madanes, Cloe. "Case 13: A Depressed Boy." in **Strategic Family Therapy,** by Cloe Madanes, 103-109. San Francisco, CA: Jossey Bass, 1984.

A thirteen-year-old boy was severely depressed, experienced fits of crying, refused to attend school, and threatened suicide. After family therapy, he attended school regularly, spent time with friends, and participated in sports.

2.086. Madanes, Cloé. "A Depressed Man: A Case Study." Chapter in **Strategic Family Therapy,** by Cloe Madanes, 178-215. San Francisco, CA: Jossey-Bass, 1984.

A sixty-year-old accountant had undergone group and individual therapy for severe depression, which had lasted several years. He was referred for marital therapy because previous therapy had been ineffective. His problem was defined as irresponsibility, rather than depression. The accountant had for years been neglecting his work. The matter was resolved after five therapeutic interventions and approximately four months' time. There is a summary of this case on pages 34-39 of the above book.

2.087. Mahler, Margaret S. "Notes on the Development of Basic Moods: The Depressive Affect." in **Psychoanalysis - A General Psychology: Essays in Honor of Heinz Hartmann,** edited by Rudolph M. Loewenstein, Lottie M. Newman, Max Schur and Albert J. Solnit, 152-168. New York, NY: International Universities Press, 1966.

2.088. Mark, Vernon H. and Jeffrey P. Mark. "Depression: The Most Common Cause of Reversible Vital Memory Loss and Intellectual Deterioration." Chapter in **Reversing Memory Loss: Proven Methods for Regaining, Strengthening, and Preserving Your Memory,** by Vernon H. Mark and Jeffrey P. Mark, 48-64. Boston, MA: Houghton Mifflin, 1992.

2.089. McGee, Mark G. and David W. Wilson. "Bipolar Disorder." in **Psychology: Science and Application,** by Mark G. McGee and David W. Wilson, 402-403. St. Paul, MN: West Publishing, 1984.

2.090. McGee, Mark G. and David W. Wilson. "Major Depressive Disorder." in **Psychology: Science and Application,** by Mark G. McGee and David W. Wilson, 401-402. St. Paul, MN: West Publishing, 1984.

2.091. McKinney, Fred. "Emerging from Feelings of Depression." in **Psychology of Personal Adjustment: Students' Introduction to Mental Hygiene,** Third Edition, by Fred McKinney, 387-396. New York, NY: John Wiley and Sons, 1960.

2.092. Mercer, Margaret. "Diagnostic Testing in Two Cases of Schizophrenic Depression." Chapter in **A Rorschach Reader,** edited by Murray H. Sherman, 67-81. New York, NY: International Universities Press, 1960.

A single white male of twenty-five was, with the aid of Rorschach testing, diagnosed as a catatonic schizophrenic, and a married white male of twenty-eight was diagnosed as a paranoid schizophrenic. Electroshock treatment (ECT) was administered to these hospitalized patients to help reveal the psychopathology underlying their respective depressive features. Analysis of test results had implications for therapy. 7 tables.

2.093. Miller, William R. and Ricardo F. Munoz. "The Ability to Deal with Depression." Chapter in **How to Control Your Drinking,** Revised Edition, by William R. Miller and Ricardo F. Munoz, 98-102. Albuquerque, NM: University of New Mexico Press, 1982.

2.094. Minkowski, Eugene. "Findings in a Case of Schizophrenic Depression." Chapter in **Existence: A New Dimension in Psychiatry and Psychology,** edited by Rollo May, Ernest Angel, and Henri F. Ellenberger, 127-138. New York, NY: Simon and Schuster, 1958.

A sixty-six-year-old man, suffering from schizophrenic depression, spoke of his guilt, punishment, and persecution. Sometimes the depressive element was dominant in this patient; sometimes the delusional and delirious element was dominant.

2.095. Mondanaro, Josette. "Depression." in **Chemically Dependent Women: Assessment and Treatment,** by Josette Mondanaro, 129-133. Lexington, MA: Lexington Books, 1989.

A forty-six-year-old woman had a variety of problems, including cocaine and alcohol dependency, and, also, hypothyroidism. She had used alcohol to balance the effect of amphetamines and cocaine. She had sought help from Alcoholics Anonymous (AA), Narcotics Anonymous (NA), an acupuncturist, a chiropractor, and other sources. This person illustrates the classic case in which treating chemical dependency was insufficient in dealing with multiple problems.

2.096. Moses, Donald A. and Robert E. Burger. "Depression of the Drug Abuser." in **Are You Driving Your Children to Drink?: Coping with Teenage Alcohol and Drug Abuse,** by Donald A. Moses and Robert E. Burger, 76-91. New York, NY: Van Nostrand Reinhold, 1975.

2.097. Myers, Michael F. "Undiagnosed Depression." in **Doctors' Marriages: A Look at the Problems and Their Solutions,** by Michael F. Myers, 63-66. New York, NY: Plenum, 1988.

When some doctors recognize depression in themselves, they do not feel "right" about contacting a psychiatrist. They feel they will be perceived as being weak or a failure. They feel a psychiatrist will judge them. These doctors do not have an informed understanding of a psychiatrist's role in helping patients.

2.098. Nadelson, Carol C., Malkah T. Notman and David W. Preven. "Case 2." in **The Impaired Physician,** edited by Stephen C. Scheiber and Brian B. Doyle, 86-87. New York, NY: Plenum, 1983.

Depression in a male medical student, who became depressed after learning his parents were getting divorced.

2.099. Norris, Ronald V. and Colleen Sullivan. "Mood Swings and Depression." Chapter in **PMS/Premenstrual Syndrome,** by Ronald V. Norris and Colleen Sullivan, 43-49. New York, NY: Rawson Associates, 1983.

Mood swings or depression are common, as a PMS (premenstrual syndrome) symptom, in women who are at the stage between ovulation and their menstrual flow. Suicides, crying spells, and admissions to hospitals increase during the last four days prior to menstruation and first four days of menstruation. Nardil and lithium carbonate appear to be effective in treating depression in PMS women. Other treatments - vitamin therapy, progesterone, exercise - are necessary to treat the PMS.

2.100. Nuwer, Hank. "Depression and Suicide." in **Steroids,** by Hank Nuwer, 63-64. New York, NY: Franklin Watts, 1990.

Deep depression is one withdrawal symptom experienced by young people, who take high doses of steroids, then stop taking them. This was noted by Dr. Kirk Brower of the University of Michigan. There have been steroid-associated suicides. A Chicago youth, being treated for depression by several doctors, hung himself. These doctors were not aware the youth was secretly using steroids. Dr. Michael Scott, a U.S. Olympic Committee physician, learned in 1989 that a bodybuilder had contracted AIDS, after sharing a needle used to inject steroids.

2.101. Nydes, Jule. "Paranoid-Masochistic Depression." in **Psychoanalysis in America: Historical Perspectives,** edited by Murray H. Sherman, 197-200. Springfield, IL: Charles C. Thomas, 1966.

2.102. O'Kelly, Lawrence I. and Frederick A. Muckler. "Involutional Melancholia." in **Introduction to Psychopathology,** Second Edition, by Lawrence I. O'Kelly and Frederick A. Muckler, 314-318. Englewood Cliffs, NJ: Prentice-Hall, 1955.

2.103. O'Kelly, Lawrence I. and Frederick A. Muckler. "Retarded Depression." in **Introduction to Psychopathology,** Second Edition, by Lawrence I. O'Kelly and Frederick A. Muckler, 308-313. Englewood Cliffs, NJ: Prentice-Hall, 1955.

The depressed person should receive competent professional help. Attempts by friends and relatives to cheerup or ignore this person increases the person's depression. Parties, trips, and visits from friends contribute to the person's problem rather than offer a solution to it.

2.104. Overstreet, H.A. "Some of Us Have Moods." Chapter in **About Ourselves: Psychology for Normal People,** by H.A. Overstreet, 108-122. New York, NY: W.W. Norton and Company, 1927.

2.105. Page, Merrill-Lynn. "Depression, Anxiety, and Suicide." Chapter in **Emergency Medicine: A Comprehensive Review,** edited by Thomas Clarke Kravis and Carmen Germaine Warner, 533-542. Rockville, MD: Aspen Systems, 1983.

2.106. Papalia, Diane E. and Sally Wendkos Olds. "Affective Disorders: Depression and Mania." in **Psychology,** by Diane E. Papalia and Sally Wendkos Olds, 532-538. New York, NY: McGraw-Hill, 1985.

Chronic physical illness or alcohol dependency can precipitate affective disorders. These disorders may have a hereditary aspect because they tend to recur in families. Even infants may become depressed. Psychiatrist Larry Pardue, after noting his own depression and depression in nineteen close relatives, believed there can be a tendency to inherit depression. 1 photograph.

2.107. Paulson, Morris J. and Dorothy Stone. "Theoretical and Clinical Issues in Severe Depression and Latency-Age Suicidal Behavior of Children." Chapter in **Pediatric Consultation Liaison Psychiatry,** edited by Charles E. Hollingsworth, 207-237. New York, NY: SP Medical and Scientific Books, 1983.

Johnny, a white male, age nine, who lived in an oppressive home and was overwhelmed with guilt - because he had violently attacked his mother and sister - attempted suicide by hanging. Mary, a white female, age eight, received severe burns after purposely scalding herself. Mary, although never rewarded when she did something well, was constantly punished when she did something poorly. Carlos, male, age eleven, was constantly punished because of statements that he wanted to kill his family. He was preoccupied with firesetting and beat himself. Carlos attempted suicide by jumping out of an upper story window to the ground. 2 tables. 47 references.

2.108. Perris, Carlo. "Cognitive Therapy with the Adult Depressed Patient." Chapter in **Comprehensive Handbook of Cognitive Therapy**, edited by Arthur Freeman, Karen M. Simon, Larry E. Beutler and Hal Arkowitz, 299-319. New York, NY: Plenum, 1989.

Depressed individuals have, according to the cognitive theory of depression, not only dysfunctional opinions of themselves, but, also, faulty cognitions. These faulty cognitions refer to errors in the perception of information. Examples include: (1) selective perception, (2) dichotomous thinking, and (3) overgeneralization. These and other cognitive errors also apply to healthy persons and to other types of patients. However, the frequency and pervasiveness of such thoughts are more pronounced in depressed individuals. 5 figures. Author biographical information. 104 references.

2.109. Porter, Frances Sarnacki, Linda Canfield Blick and Suzanne M. Sgroi. "Depression." in **Handbook of Clinical Intervention in Child Sexual Abuse**, by Suzanne M. Sgroi, 118-119. Lexington, MA: Lexington Books, 1982.

A nine-year-old male, sexually abused by his uncle, attempted suicide by hanging. A female, pregnant by her father, tried to kill herself and the unborn baby. There are signs of depression in almost all child victims of sexual abuse, after the victims disclose the abuse.

2.110. Reus, Victor I. "Mood Disorders." Chapter in **Review of General Psychiatry**, Third Edition, edited by Howard H. Goldman, 226-241. Norwalk, CT: Appleton and Lange, 1992.

Genetic, biochemical, neuroendocrinological, and other research indicates most mood disorders have a biological basis. It is often noted in clinical practice the boundaries between different disorders are not distinct. 1 table. 28 references.

2.111. Rosanoff, Aaron J. "Involutional Melancholia." Chapter in **An Outline of Abnormal Psychology**, edited by Gardner Murphy, 129-135. New York, NY: Modern Library, 1929.

2.112. Rosenbaum, Jerrold F. and James E. Groves. "Depression and Grief." in **Massachusetts General Hospital Handbook of General Hospital Psychiatry**, Third Edition, edited by Ned H. Cassem, 438. St. Louis, MO: Mosby Year Book, 1991.

2.113. Rothstein, Arnold. "Dolly: A Depressed Neurotic Suppliant Personality Disorder." Chapter in **The Narcissistic Pursuit of Perfection**, by Arnold Rothstein, 165-170. New York, NY: International Universities Press, 1980.

2.114. Ruch, Floyd L. "Depressive and Manic Episodes." in **Psychology and Life**, Seventh Edition, by Floyd L. Ruch, 488-489. Glenview, IL: Scott, Foresman and Company, 1967.

2.115. Ruch, Floyd L. "Depressive Reaction." in **Psychology and Life**, Seventh Edition, by Floyd L. Ruch, 484-485. Glenview, IL: Scott, Foresman and Company, 1967.

2.116. Salzberger-Wittenberg, Isca. "Depressive Anxieties and Defences against Them in Adult, Child and Infant." Chapter in **Psycho-Analytic Insight and Relationships: A Kleinian Approach**, by Isca Salzberger-Wittenberg, 64-85. London: Routledge and Kegan Paul, 1970.

2.117. Samuels, Susan K. and Susana Sikorsky. "Major Depressive Episode." in **Clinical Evaluations of School-Aged Children: A Structured Approach to the Diagnosis of Child and Adolescent Mental Disorders**, by Susan K. Samuels and Susana Sikorsky, 86-91. Sarasota, FL: Professional Resource Exchange, 1990.

A major depressive episode/dysthymia interview form - in this instance consisting of seventeen questions - is useful in diagnosing major depressive episode. A Checklist consisting of key concepts such as impulsivity, aggressiveness, anxiety, cognition, and others can also be useful. 7 references.

2.118. Schmidt, David D. and Edward Messner. "Depression." in **Behavioral Science in Family Practice**, by Gerald M. Rosen, John P. Geyman and Richard H. Layton, 127-129. New York, NY: Appleton-Century-Crofts, 1980.

2.119. Shaw, Brian F. and Aaron T. Beck. "The Treatment of Depression with Cognitive Therapy." Chapter in **Handbook of Rational-Emotive Therapy**, by Albert Ellis and Russell Grieger, 309-326. New York, NY: Springer, 1977.

2.120. Sifneos, Peter E. "Man Complaining of Depression: An Evaluation Interview." Chapter in **Short-Term Anxiety-Provoking Psychotherapy: A Treatment Manual**, by Peter E. Sifneos, 78-88. N.p., Basic Books, 1992.

2.121. Speller, Jeffrey Lynn. "Down and Almost Out: The Story of a Depressed Executive." Chapter in **Executives in Crisis: Recognizing and Managing the Alcoholic, Drug-Addicted, or Mentally Ill Executive,** by Jeffrey Lynn Speller, 50-62. San Francisco, CA: Jossey-Bass, 1989.

2.122. Speller, Jeffrey Lynn. "Soaring: The Story of a Manic Executive." Chapter in **Executives in Crisis: Recognizing and Managing the Alcoholic, Drug-Addicted, or Mentally Ill Executive,** by Jeffrey Lynn Speller, 63-73. San Francisco, CA: Jossey-Bass, 1989.

2.123. Starr, Adaline. "Working with Depression." Chapter in **Rehearsal for Living: Psychodrama: Illustrated Therapeutic Techniques,** by Adaline Starr, 303-328. Chicago, IL: Nelson Hall, 1977.

2.124. Surman, Owen S. "Major Depressive Disorder." in **Massachusetts General Hospital Handbook of General Hospital Psychiatry,** Third Edition, edited by Ned H. Cassem, 77-78. St. Louis, MO: Mosby Year Book, 1991.

2.125. Taylor, Robert L. "Depression." in **Mind or Body: Distinguishing Psychological from Organic Disorders,** by Robert L. Taylor, 34-37. New York, NY: McGraw-Hill, 1982.

Personal loss is not always the causative factor in depression. A person who is organically ill may also experience a personal loss. This personal loss may not be etiologically significant regarding the person's depression. A twenty-nine-year-old woman stated at a psychiatric clinic she was depressed. Her father had killed himself; her mother had experienced involutional depressive psychosis. The twenty-nine-year-old woman was also depressed after the birth of her second child and after she began taking birth control pills. Her depression disappeared after she stopped taking these pills.

2.126. Thomas, R. Murray. "Counseling Depressed Clients." in **Counseling and Life-Span Development,** by R. Murray Thomas, 313-316. Newbury Park, CA: Sage, 1990.

A treatment approach for depressed older adults should take into account a number of factors, including client health, financial status, social support patterns, and potential interests.

2.127. Tilley, Barbara W. "Counseling Depressed Clients." Chapter in **Short-Term Counseling: A Psychoanalytic Approach,** by Barbara W. Tilley, 235-258. New York, NY: International Universities Press, 1984.

Chemically depressed individuals seek from others continual attention. They are never convinced they are loved or successful, the reason being they never developed during infancy sufficient self-esteem. They may seem unable to love because they are more likely concerned with being loved. They express hostility and obtain revenge by making others feel uncomfortable and guilty. The depressed often resort to drugs, alcohol, excessive eating, or anorexia to soothe pain and fight emptiness. Suicidal impulses may be acted out through drugs, alcohol, or frequent accidents. 3 references.

2.128. Tolbert, Herman A. and L. Eugene Arnold. "Adolescent Adjustment Disorder with Depressed Mood." in **Behavioral Problems in Childhood: A Primary Care Approach,** edited by Stewart Gabel, 160-161. New York, NY: Grune and Stratton, 1981.

Dyspepsia, anorexia, constipation, boredom, and a need for constant pleasure/stimulation are features in depression.

2.129. Wadeson, Harriet. "Depression." Chapter in **Art Psychotherapy,** by Harriet Wadeson, 46-67. New York, NY: John Wiley and Sons, 1980.

2.130. Wadeson, Harriet. "Manic-Depressive Psychosis." Chapter in **Art Psychotherapy,** by Harriet Wadeson, 68-81. New York, NY: John Wiley and Sons, 1980.

2.131. Walker, J. Ingram. "Depression (Singing the Blues and How to Stop)." Chapter in **Everybody's Guide to Emotional Well-Being: Helping Yourself Get Help,** by J. Ingram Walker, 39-60. San Francisco, CA: Harbor Publishing, 1982.

Although there are approximately 25,000 suicides annually in the U.S., there are probably twice as many as this which are misclassified and unreported. There is a suicide in the U.S. every twenty minutes. Suicide is the leading cause of death for physicians under age forty.

2.132. Wanigaratne, Shamil, Wendy Wallace, Jane Pullin, Francis Keaney and Roger Farmer. "Depression." Chapter in **Relapse Prevention for Addictive Behaviours: A Manual for**

Therapists, by Shamil Wanigaratne, Wendy Wallace, Jane Pullin, Francis Keaney and Roger Farmer, 151-159. Oxford: Blackwell Scientific, 1990.

2.133. Weeks, Gerald R. and Luciano L'Abate. "Case 2: Paradoxical Treatment of Depression." in **Paradoxical Psychotherapy: Theory and Practice with Individuals, Couples, and Families,** by Gerald R. Weeks and Luciano L'Abate, 202-210. New York, NY: Brunner/Mazel, 1982.

Paradoxical treatment was successful in the treatment of a sixty-seven-year-old white, married male, who had a long history of depression. The patient had received treatment for at least thirty years, having been twenty-three when he was first hospitalized. His treatment had included electroconvulsive treatment (ECT).

2.134. Weeks, Gerald R. and Luciano L'Abate. "The Paradoxical Treatment of Depression." in **Paradoxical Psychotherapy: Theory and Practice with Individuals, Couples and Families,** by Gerald R. Weeks and Luciano L'Abate, 145-149. New York, NY: Brunner/Mazel, 1982.

Paradoxical interventions were used to treat depression in a married, fifty-eight-year-old male, whose depression followed his second stroke. After the patient's wife changed her role from that of someone who was to help him to someone who required help, the husband's role changed from patient to rescuer. He began to do more for himself and her. After his wife and family were overly sympathetic, exaggerating their concern, the husband became more determined to increase his self-reliance.

2.135. Weiner, Irving B. "Affective Disorder: Depression and Mania." Chapter in **Child and Adolescent Psychopathology,** by Irving B. Weiner, 262-297. New York, NY: John Wiley and Sons, 1982.

2.136. Weissman, Myrna M. and Eugene S. Paykel. "Moving and Depression in Women." in **Loneliness: The Experience of Emotional and Social Isolation,** by Robert S. Weiss, 154-164. Cambridge, MA: MIT Press, 1973.

Persons who move can lose a number of things, including important social ties and familiar living patterns. These losses can contribute to depression. Depressed women in New Haven, Connecticut attributed their depression to personal problems, rather than to recent moves. These women, in doing this, internalized stresses and became depressed. That the moves were voluntary and related to, for example, improved housing did not prevent depression.

2.137. Wekstein, Louis. "Somatization, Masked Depression and Self-Destruction." in **Handbook of Suicidology: Principles, Problems, and Practice,** by Louis Wekstein, 262-268. New York, NY: Brunner/Mazel, 1979.

2.138. Wender, Paul H. and Donald F. Klein. "Manic States." in **Mind, Mood, and Medicine: A Guide to the New Biopsychiatry,** by Paul H. Wender and Donald F. Klein, 54-58. New York, NY: Farrar · Straus-Giroux, 1981.

Psychiatric diagnoses cannot be made on the basis of laboratory tests because no such tests exist. Mood shifts cannot be explained strictly in psychological or biological terms. Signs and symptoms, however, can be used to infer an illness.

2.139. Wender, Paul H. and Donald F. Klein. "Masked Depression." in **Mind, Mood, and Medicine: A Guide to the New Biopsychiatry,** by Paul H. Wender and Donald F. Klein, 63-66. New York, NY: Farrar · Straus - Giroux, 1981.

2.140. Wender, Paul H. and Donald F. Klein. "Nonvital Depression: Neurotic Depression and Depressive Character." in **Mind, Mood, and Medicine: A Guide to the New Biopsychiatry,** by Paul H. Wender and Donald F. Klein, 58-63. New York, NY: Farrar · Straus - Giroux, 1981.

2.141. Wender, Paul H. and Donald F. Klein. "Vital Depression." in **Mind, Mood, and Medicine: A Guide to the New Biopsychiatry,** by Paul H. Wender and Donald F. Klein, 43-53. New York, NY: Farrar · Straus - Giroux, 1981.

Guilt is a characteristic of depressed persons in Western Judeo-Christian society. Guilt is rare in depressed persons in Asia and Africa, with the exception of Westernized individuals. It appears that culture - not illness - accounts for the presence or absence of guilt.

2.142. White, Robert W. "Depressive and Manic Disorders." Chapter in **The Abnormal Personality,** by Robert W. White, 513-543. New York, NY: Ronald Press, 1956.

Clifford W. Beers discussed in his autobiography, **A Mind That Found Itself,** published in 1931, his three years of manic and depressive experiences.

2.143. Wicks, Robert J. "Depression and Anger." in **Helping Others: Ways of Listening, Sharing and Counseling,** by Robert J. Wicks, 117-121. Radnor, PA: Chilton Book Company, 1979.

2.144. Wishnie, Howard. "Depression." in **The Impulsive Personality: Understanding People with Destructive Character Disorders,** by Howard Wishnie, 40-67. New York, NY: Plenum, 1977.

2.145. Wishnie, Howard. "Examples of Depression." in **The Impulsive Personality: Understanding People with Destructive Character Disorders,** by Howard Wishnie, 67-70. New York, NY: Plenum, 1977.

2.146. Wolpe, Joseph. "Transcript of Initial Interview in a Case of Depression." Chapter in **Behavior Modification Procedure: A Sourcebook,** edited by Edwin J. Thomas, 152-162. Chicago, IL: Aldine, 1974.

A one-hour-long interview can be recorded, and used as a consultation-demonstration, for psychiatric residents to illustrate external and internal stimulus conditions that elicit neurotic responses. A depressed, forty-one-year old married woman is the interviewee. 1 reference.

2.147. Young, Patrick. "Depression and Mania." Chapter in **Mental Disturbances,** by Patrick Young, 23-35. New York, NY: Chelsea House Publishers, 1988.

GOVERNMENT DOCUMENTS AND ASSOCIATION PUBLICATIONS

2.148. Sargent, Marilyn. **Depressive Illnesses: Treatments Bring New Hope.** Rockville, MD: National Institute of Mental Health, 1989. DHHS Publication No. (ADM) 89-1491.

In the U.S., during any six-month period, approximately 10 million people have a depressive illness. The cost emotionally and economically to Americans is huge. Economic costs alone may be annually as high as $16 billion. The cost in human suffering is incalcuable. It is estimated that appropriate treatment can alleviate nearly 80% of serious depressions.

CHAPTERS AND SECTIONS IN GOVERNMENT DOCUMENTS AND ASSOCIATION PUBLICATIONS

2.149. Andreasen, Nancy C. and Donald W. Black. "Mood (Affective) Disorders." Chapter in **Introductory Textbook of Psychiatry,** by Nancy C. Andreasen and Donald W. Black, 189-225. Washington, DC: American Psychiatric Press, 1991.

Perhaps the oldest recorded example of mood disorder is in the Ebers papyrus, a medical document found in ancient Egypt. There are throughout history many examples of famous individuals who suffered from disorders of mood. St. Augustine, John Berryman, Ernest Hemingway, William James, John Keats, Robert Lowell, Sylvia Plath, Anne Sexton, and Leo Tolstoy are nine of these persons. 11 tables. 2 figures. 55 references. 12 self-assessment questions.

2.150. Silver, Larry B. "Depression." in **Attention-Deficit Hyperactivity Disorder: A Clinical Guide to Diagnosis and Treatment,** by Larry B. Silver, 19-20. Washington, DC: American Psychiatric Press, 1992.

2.151. Skodol, Andrew E. "Mood Disturbances." Chapter in **Problems in Differential Diagnosis: From DSM-III to DSM-III-R in Clinical Practice,** by Andrew E. Skodol, 221-274. Washington, DC: American Psychiatric Press, 1989.

Chapter 3

TREATMENT OPTIONS

BOOKS FOR PROFESSIONALS AND THE GENERAL PUBLIC

3.001. Badal, Daniel W. **Treatment of Depression and Related Moods: A Manual for Psychotherapists.** London: Jason Aronson, 1988.

3.002. Beach, Steven R.H., Evelyn E. Sandeen and K. Daniel O'Leary. **Depression in Marriage: A Model for Etiology and Treatment.** New York, NY: Guilford Press, 1990.

According to David H. Barlow, the editor of **Treatment Manuals for Practitioners,** of which **Depression in Marriage: A Model for Etiology and Treatment** is one volume, 50% of depressed women have marital difficulties and 50% of women who have marital problems are depressed. The Marital Therapy Scale consists of three parts: (1) Therapist Technical Marital Therapy Skills (30-item checklist), (2) Therapist General Therapy Skills (18-item checklist), and (3) Additional Considerations (3-item checklist).

3.003. Breggin, Peter Roger. **Electroshock: Its Brain-Disabling Effects.** New York, NY: Springer, 1979.

Dr. Breggin is a psychiatrist and the founder and executive director, Center for the Study of Psychiatry. He believes that up to 100,000 persons annually are administered ECT (electroconvulsive therapy). Some of the results of this treatment: confusion, impaired judgement, and amnesia. Human autopsy studies, animal research, and anecdotal accounts indicate ECT brain damage.

3.004. Cleve, Jay. **Out of the Blues: Strategies That Work to Get You through the Down Times.** Minneapolis, MN: CompCare, 1989.

Dr. Jay Cleve conducts seminars and workshops on depression management.

3.005. Davidson, Park O. Editor. **The Behavioral Management of Anxiety, Depression and Pain.** New York, NY: Brunner/Mazel, 1976.

Papers were presented in 1975 in Banff, Alberta, at the Banff International Conference on Behavior Modification, and formed the basis for this book. The contributors to the book: (1) Anthony Biglan, (2) Wilbert E. Fordyce, (3) Peter M. Lewinsohn, (4) Peter McLean, (5) Donald Meichenbaum, (6) Ernest G. Poser, (7) Dennis Turk, and (8) Antonette M. Zeiss.

3.006. Flach, Frederic F. and Suzanne C. Draghi. **The Nature and Treatment of Depression.** New York, NY: John Wiley and Sons, 1975.

3.007. Gershon, Samuel and Baron Shopsin. Editors. **Lithium: Its Role in Psychiatric Research and Treatment.** New York, NY: Plenum, 1973.

The lithium ion was introduced as a psychoactive drug in 1949. Psychiatrists at this time did not routinely treat psychological problems with pharmacological methods. There were toxic hazards to contend with and the deaths due to lithium of some patients. Lithium's ready availability was the reason why drug companies virtually ignored it. Rowell Laboratories in Baudette, Minnesota was the exception. This company began to commercially market lithium in 1969.

3.008. Kline, Nathan S. **From Sad to Glad: Kline on Depression.** New York, NY: Ballantine Books, 1974.

Dr. Nathan S. Kline received two Lasker Awards for his research in antidepressant medication. The SAD-GLAD Scale is used to evaluate depression. SAD stands for "systematic assessment of depression." GLAD stands for "graduated linear assessment of delight." Mood; anxiety; sleep; appetite and weight change; memory; and guilt are some of the variables rated by the SAD-GLAD Scale. 1 diagram. 1 graph.

3.009. Marmorstein, Jerome and Nanette Marmorstein. **The Psychometabolic Blues.** Santa Barbara, CA: Woodbridge, 1979.

3.010. Nezu, Arthur M., Christine M. Nezu and Michael G. Perri. **Problem-Solving Therapy for Depression: Theory, Research, and Clinical Guidelines.** New York, NY: John Wiley and Sons, 1989.

Appendix A, "Format of Problem-Solving Group Treatment for a 10-Week Program," lists ten sessions and the components of each session. The first session consists of six components which are about the program's introduction and rationale. The fifth session (eight components) pertains to decision-making (DM) training. Appendix B, "Patient Handout," discusses the philosophy of the program and problem-solving processes.

3.011. Rehm, Lynn P. Editor. **Behavior Therapy for Depression: Present Status and Future Directions.** New York, NY: Academic Press, 1981.

The roots of a behavioral-model explanation for depression go back to 1928, and an article published in that year, in the **Journal of Nervous and Mental Diseases.** When a physician by the name of A.G. Ivanov-Smolensky noted that a dog, being used in a classical conditioning experiment, was unable to make a complex discrimination, Ivanov-Smolensky speculated on the parallel between the dog's behavior and the symptoms/etiology of human depression. It was to be almost forty years before behavioral models were to again be associated with depression.

3.012. Ross, Harvey M. **Fighting Depression.** New York, NY: Larchmont Books, 1975.

Although Dr. Harvey M. Ross used various methods to treat depression, he became impressed with megavitamin therapy as advocated by Dr. Allan Cott, a megavitamin therapist. Dr. Ross, skeptical at first, learned later that many schizophrenic symptoms returned, within twenty-four to forty-eight hours after certain patients stopped taking the vitamins or gave up suggested diets. Dr. Ross does not oppose the use of tranquilizers and electroconvulsive treatment (ECT). He believes that many health science professionals unjustifiably ignore megavitamin therapy.

3.013. Rush, A. John. Editor. **Short-Term Psychotherapies for Depression: Behavioral, Interpersonal, Cognitive, and Psychodynamic Approaches.** New York, NY: Guilford Press, 1982.

3.014. Sutherland Learning Associates. **Depression Today: Confident Clinical Office Management, Part Two: Managing the Acute Episode and Follow-Up Phase.** New York, NY: C.M.E. Communications, 1978.

3.015. Williams, J. Mark G. **The Psychological Treatment of Depression: A Guide to the Theory and Practice of Cognitive-Behaviour Therapy.** London: Croom Helm, 1984.

Behavioral and cognitive approaches were first used to treat clinical depression during the late 1960s and early 1970s. Combinations of these techniques appear to be more effective in reducing the strength of depression than the use of only one of the techniques. The author presented, between 1979 and 1982, seminars and workshops at the University of Newcastle-upon-Tyne Department of Psychiatry. This book evolved from the seminars and workshops.

CHAPTERS AND SECTIONS IN BOOKS FOR PROFESSIONALS AND THE GENERAL PUBLIC

3.016. Andrews, Lewis M. "Beyond Depression." Chapter in **To Thine Own Self Be True: The Relationship between Spiritual Values and Emotional Health,** by Lewis M. Andrews, 23-36. New York, NY: Doubleday, 1989.

The National Institute of Mental Health attempted, in a study called the Treatment of Depression Collaborative Research Program (TDCRP), to compare the effectiveness of psychotherapy with psychoactive drugs in the treatment of depression. This study involved, in part, over six years, 239 patients, twenty-eight therapists, five universities, and a budget of $10 million. The study outcome: talk therapies were at least as effective as drug therapy. Dr. Thomas Hora advises depressed patients to rid themselves of malicious thoughts. These thoughts harm only the patients - not the persons against whom the thoughts are directed. William James, the nineteenth-century psychologist, gave the example of Horace Fletcher, a writer who could easily curb his resentful habits, this ability likely contributing to Fletcher's mental health.

3.017. Barker, Philip. "Metaphors for Depressed People." in **Using Metaphors in Psychotherapy,** by Philip Barker, 125-126. New York, NY: Brunner/Mazel, 1985.

A variety of metaphors, ranging from religious to business themes, can be used to treat some depressed persons.

3.018. Bartlett, Steven J. "Treating Depression." in **When You Don't Know Where to Turn: A Self-Diagnosing Guide to Counseling and Therapy,** by Steven J. Bartlett, 208-210. Chicago, IL: Contemporary Books, 1987.

According to Dr. Thaddeus Kostrubala, the chronically depressed person can often reduce, even eliminate, through long distance running, early morning awakening and insomnia. Although running can increase independence and self-confidence, psychotherapy and drug therapy can encourage dependency on the therapist. Even ten minutes of rigorous exercise doubles the normal amount of the hormone epinephrine. Dr. Malcolm Carruthers, leader of a British medical group, studied epinephrine. This hormone counteracts depression. Psychiatrist John H. Greist, University of Wisconsin, learned that some seriously depressed persons benefitted more from therapeutic running than did others from traditional therapy.

3.019. Bell, Iris R. and Alan J. Gelenberg. "Mood Disorders." in **Conn's Current Therapy: Latest Approved Methods of Treatment for the Practicing Physician,** edited by Robert E. Rakel, 1113-1122. Philadelphia, PA: W.B. Saunders, 1993.

3.020. Belsky, Janet K. "Are You Depressed?" in **Here Tomorrow: Making the Most of Life after Fifty,** by Janet K. Belsky, 76-80. Baltimore, MD: Johns Hopkins University Press, 1988.

Hypothyroidism, Cushing's disease, uremia, and leukemia are a few illnesses characterized, in part, by depression. Psychotherapy is the preferred treatment when an external, situational, cause produces depression. Psychotherapy would be preferred for a person whose spouse has died. Medication is the preferred treatment for someone who has a brain chemistry defect. 1 table.

3.021. Berger, F.M. "Depression." in **Drug Treatment of Mental Disorders,** edited by Lance L. Simpson, 95-96. New York, NY: Raven, 1976.

It was learned at a large municipal hospital that 16% of 365 neurotic outpatients were anxious; 5% of the 365 outpatients were depressed.

3.022. Bernstein, Jerrold G. "Depression." in **Massachusetts General Hospital Handbook of General Hospital Psychiatry,** Third Edition, edited by Ned H. Cassem, 538-539. St. Louis, MO: Mosby Year Book, 1991.

3.023. Bernstein, Jerrold G. "Manic States." in **Massachusetts General Hospital Handbook of General Hospital Psychiatry,** Third Edition, edited by Ned H. Cassem, 538. St. Louis, MO: Mosby Year Book, 1991.

Lithium carbonate, haloperidol, and chlorpromazine can be used to treat manic states. Lithium carbonate acts slowly and requires up to two weeks to be effective. Haloperidol acts more rapidly and is effective in one to three days. Chlorpromazine may sedate the patient and not improve the manic nature of the patient's behavior.

3.024. Blazer, Dan G., II. "Depression." Chapter in **The Merck Manual of Geriatrics,** 1014-1018. Rahway, NJ: Merck Sharp and Dohme Research Laboratories, 1990.

Nortriptyline, desipramine, and doxepin are widely used in treating depressed elderly persons. Drugs which produce the least number of or least severe side effects are preferred for these persons. Electroconvulsive therapy (ECT) is used to treat individuals on whom tricyclic antidepressants do not have any effect. ECT is as affective in treating the elderly as it is in treating younger patients. The figure in most studies is 80%. 1 table.

3.025. Branden, Nathaniel. "Anxiety and Depression." in **The Psychology of Self-Esteem: A New Concept of Man's Psychological Nature,** by Nathaniel Branden, 168-172. New York, NY: Bantam Books, 1969.

Depressed persons regain their mental health after they confront their anxiety-provoking conflicts. These persons have to resolve their conflicts. Depression is acceptance of defeat.

3.026. Byyny, Richard L. and Leon Speroff. "Depression and Dementia." Chapter in **A Clinical Guide for the Care of Older Women,** by Richard L. Byyny and Leon Speroff, 299-306. Baltimore, MD: Williams and Wilkins, 1990.

3.027. Cassem, Ned H. "Depression." Chapter in **Massachusetts General Hospital Handbook of General Hospital Psychiatry,** Third Edition, edited by Ned H. Cassem, 237-268. St. Louis, MO: Mosby Year Book, 1991.

Depression, particularly major depression, can have very serious negative effects on inpatients and outpatients, who have a heart condition. These depressed individuals may be proceeding to cardiac surgery or may have had a heart attack during the previous twenty-four hours. In either case, depression increases the chances of other heart attacks - even death. 8 tables. 1 figure. 108 references.

3.028. Cassem, Ned H. and Thomas P. Hackett. "Major Depression and Despondency." in **Massachusetts General Hospital Handbook of General Hospital Psychiatry,** Third Edition, edited by Ned H. Cassem, 390. St. Louis, MO: Mosby Year Book, 1991.

3.029. Coon, Dennis. "Coping with Death and Depression - Problems for Everyone." in **Introduction to Psychology: Exploration and Application,** Third Edition, by Dennis Coon, 308-311. St. Paul, MN: West Publishing, 1983.

3.030. Corey, Gerald. "Theme: Dealing with Depression." in **Theory and Practice of Group Counseling,** Second Edition, by Gerald Corey, 437-439. Monterey, CA: Brooks/Cole, 1985.

Person-centered, psychoanalytic, reality-therapy, and transactional-analysis perspectives can be applied to helping a divorced alcoholic.

3.031. Corey, Gerald. "Treatment of Depression." in **Theory and Practice of Counseling and Psychotherapy,** Third Edition, by Gerald Corey, 228-230. Monterey, CA: Brooks/Cole, 1986.

3.032. Craddock, Denis. "Drug Treatment." in **A Short Textbook of General Practice,** Third Edition, by Denis Craddock, 374-379. London: H.K. Lewis, 1976.

Clomipramine (Anafranil), one of the tricyclic antidepressants, is effective against depression, if the depression is accompanied by a pronounced phobic element. Tranylcypromine (Parnate) is the most powerful monoamine oxidase inhibitor. Lithium should not be used during the first trimester of pregnancy.

3.033. Curry, Hiram B. "Depression." in **Behavioral Science in Family Practice,** by Gerald M. Rosen, John P. Geyman and Richard H. Layton, 167-169. New York, NY: Appleton-Century-Crofts, 1980.

A physician can, to help a depressed patient, move closer to the patient. This will symbolize the physician's willingness to share the patient's problem. The physician can reinforce this gesture by touching the patient. The physician can encourage the patient to behave as the patient feels. Crying can ventilate pent-up feelings.

3.034. Davis, Donald I. "Violence, Mania and Depression." in **Alcoholism Treatment: An Integrative Family and Individual**

Approach, by Donald I. Davis, 144-146. New York, NY: Gardner, 1987.

Dr. Kenneth Williams administered lithium carbonate, in the late 1970s, to alcoholics who exhibited severely violent or destructive behavior, when they drank. Dr. Williams at that time was at the University of Pittsburgh, where he was head of an alcoholism treatment program. Dr. Donald I. Davis noted a mellowing of affect in several men. This was after these men were administered for one or two days one or two 300 mg lithium carbonate tablets. The men reported experiencing an internal calming. Some manic and alcoholic persons who are treated with lithium to control their mania, and respond well, can also abstain more easily from drinking.

3.035. Davis, John M. "Tricyclic Antidepressants." Chapter in **Drug Treatment of Mental Disorders**, edited by Lance L. Simpson, 127-146. New York, NY: Raven, 1976.

Prior to the late 1950s, psychotherapy, narcotics, and electroconvulsive therapy (ECT) were some of the main methods of treating depression. In general, severe psychotics or endogenous depressives respond best to tricyclic drugs. These drugs help approximately 70% of depressives. 1 table. 2 figures. 22 references.

3.036. Dean, Herbert M. and John J. Massarelli. "Depression." in **Look to Your Health: What You Should Know about the Body, Common Diseases, and Healthful Living**, by Herbert M. Dean and John J. Massarelli, 283-287. New York, NY: Van Nostrand Reinhold, 1980.

Amines are chemicals found in the brain. Many depressed persons have a decreased amount of amines. Reserpine, a high blood pressure medication, can reduce the amount of amines, and a person can become depressed. Dopa, another drug, can reverse the loss of amines and can, thus, counter depression. Iproniazid is an effective antidepressant because it increases the amount of amines. Imipramine increases the effects of amines.

3.037. "Depression: 22 Ways to Beat the Blues." in **The Doctors Book of Home Remedies: Thousands of Tips and Techniques Anyone Can Use to Heal Everyday Health Problems**, edited by Debora Tkac, 203-209. New York, NY: Bantam Books, 1991.

Talk to a trusted friend. Have a warm bath. Get a massage. Exercise. Activity is the keyword.

3.038. Dowling, Colette. "Food Restrictions for Patients on MAO Inhibitors." Appendix in **You Mean I Don't Have to Feel This Way?: New Help for Depression, Anxiety, and Addiction,** by Colette Dowling, 245-246. New York, NY: Charles Scribner's Sons, 1991.

Summer sausage, salami, vermouth, brandy, overripe figs, and overripe bananas are examples of foods and beverages that must be avoided completely by individuals on MAOI (monoamine oxidase inhibitor) medication. Beer, sour cream, avocados, and sauerkraut are some of the foods and beverages that should be used in moderation by these persons. The preceding instructions must also be adhered to for two weeks after ceasing to take MAOIs. Medications with stimulant properties - for example, cocaine and amphetamines - should be avoided, as should other opiate narcotics, for instance, demerol (Meperidine) and dextromethorphan (DM).

3.039. Emery, Gary and James Campbell. "Let Go of Depression and Create Self-Esteem." Chapter in **Rapid Relief from Emotional Distress,** by Gary Emery and James Campbell, 149-165. New York, NY: Fawcett Columbine, 1986.

Demoralization, helplessness, and hopelessness usually precede depression, depression being synonymous with low self-esteem. Overthinking and underacting maintain depression. Relabeling enables a person to see more - not less - reality. An event is experienced according to the label placed on it. If reality is labeled negatively, misery is generated. Thinking in terms of choice enables a person to label reality to their advantage.

3.040. Fieve, Ronald R. "Therapeutic Action in Depression." in **Drug Treatment of Mental Disorders,** edited by Lance L. Simpson, 196-197. New York, NY: Raven, 1976.

Lithium has been more effective than electroconvulsive therapy (ECT) in the treatment of depression.

3.041. Forrest, Gary G. "The Effect of Group Psychotherapy Upon Levels of Anxiety, Depression and Hostility within an Alcoholic Population." Chapter in **The Diagnosis and Treatment of Alcoholism,** Second Edition, by Gary G. Forrest, 311-320. Springfield, IL: Charles C. Thomas, 1978.

Thirty-five active duty military personnel, who were problem drinkers, underwent treatment at the Fort Gordon Alcoholic Rehabilitation Center. The subjects, all of whom were male, ranged in age from twenty-five to forty-four years. The twenty subjects in the experimental group received group psychotherapy; the fifteen subjects in the control group did not receive any group psychotherapy. The Multiple Affect Adjective Check List (MAACL) was self-administered to the subjects to measure anxiety, depression, and hostility. After approximately four months, therapy was completed and both groups were again tested with the MAACL. Group psychotherapy was effective in rehabilitating alcoholics by significantly reducing levels of anxiety and depression, but not significantly reducing hostility. Patients who did not receive group psychotherapy became more anxious, depressed, and hostile. 3 tables.

3.042. Gelder, Michael, Dennis Gath and Richard Mayou. "Cognitive-Behaviour Therapy for Depressive Disorders." in **Oxford Textbook of Psychiatry,** Second Edition, by Michael Gelder, Dennis Gath and Richard Mayou, 736-737. Oxford: Oxford University Press, 1989.

3.043. Goleman, Daniel and Jonathan Freedman. "Cures for Depression." in **What Psychology Knows That Everyone Should,** by Daniel Goleman and Jonathan Freedman, 230-231. Lexington, MA: Lewis Publishing, 1981.

Extreme depression can be effectively treated with electroconvulsive therapy (ECT), sometimes called electroshock. From seventy to 130 volts are administered through electrodes to the patient's temples. A seizure and brief coma result. Disorientation is a side effect. Brain damage can occur.

3.044. Graham, P.J. "Childhood Depression." in **Children in Health and Disease,** by Frederic Brimblecombe and Donald Barltrop, 472. London: Baillière Tindall, 1978.

The antidepressants imipramine and amitriptyline can be used to treat depression in children. Drowsiness and dry mouth are side effects of this medication. Electroconvulsive therapy (ECT) is rarely used for treating children. It takes a few weeks for most children to improve.

3.045. Grinspoon, Lester and James B. Bakalar. "Depression." in **Dealing with Drugs: Consequences of Government Control,** edited by Ronald Hamowy, 196-198. Lexington, MA: Lexington Books, 1987.

Amphetamines were among the first classes of drugs used in treating depression. Although that was in 1936, amphetamines were still strongly recommended more than two decades later in 1958. This was according to **The Amphetamines: Their Actions and Uses** by C.D. Leake (1958). Presently, the most effective drugs used in treating depression are tricyclic derivatives, lithium for manic-depressive illness. Psychotherapy - not drugs - should be used for mild depression.

3.046. Helfer, Mary Edna. "Understanding Anger and Depression During the Interview." in **The Battered Child,** Fourth Edition, edited by Ray E. Helfer and Ruth S. Kempe, 119-121. Chicago, IL: University of Chicago Press, 1987.

3.047. Hendler, Nelson H. and Judith Alsofrom Fenton. "Depression and Drugs." in **Coping with Chronic Pain,** by Nelson H. Hendler and Judith Alsofrom Fenton, 118-127. New York, NY: Clarkson N. Potter, 1979.

Serotonin and norepinephrine are chemicals found in the brain. If the amount of either chemical is reduced, depression will result. The administration of high blood pressure medication can reduce levels of serotonin and norepinephrine. Depression can also be caused by chemicals which inhibit the release of serotonin, Valium being one example. Tricyclic antidepressants reduce depression by increasing in the brain serotonin, norepinephrine and dopamine.

3.048. Hollon, Steven D. and Aaron T. Beck. "Cognitive Therapy of Depression." Chapter in **Cognitive-Behavioral Interventions: Theory, Research, and Procedures,** edited by Philip C. Kendall and Steven D. Hollon, 153-203. New York, NY: Academic Press, 1979.

3.049. Hosford, Ray E., Gretchen Fall Burnett and Michael E. Mills. "Depression: Current Diagnoses and Prescriptions." in **Handbook of Counseling Psychology,** edited by Steven D. Brown and Robert W. Lent, 284-301. New York, NY: John Wiley and Sons, 1984.

3.050. Ivey, Allen E. "Depression." in **Developmental Strategies for Helpers: Individual, Family, and Network Interventions,** by Allen E. Ivey, 184-185. Pacific Grove, CA: Brooks/Cole, 1991.

3.051. Kaplan, Harold I. and Benjamin J. Sadock. "Drugs Used to Treat Bipolar Disorder." in **Synopsis of Psychiatry: Behavioral Sciences, Clinical Psychiatry,** Fifth Edition, by Harold I.

Kaplan and Benjamin J. Sadock, 518-522. Baltimore, MD: Williams and Wilkins, 1988.

Drugs used to treat bipolar disorder include: (1) lithium; (2) carbamazepine and sodium valproate, both anticonvulsants; (3) levothyroxine; (4) verapamil, a calcium channel inhibitor; and (5) clonazepam, a benzodiazepine anticonvulsant. 1 table. 1 figure. 13 references.

3.052. Kaplan, Harold I. and Benjamin J. Sadock. "Drugs Used to Treat Depression." in **Synopsis of Psychiatry: Behavioral Sciences, Clinical Psychiatry,** Fifth Edition, by Harold I. Kaplan and Benjamin J. Sadock, 510-517. Baltimore, MD: Williams and Wilkins, 1988.

3.053. Kart, Cary S., Eileen S. Metress and James F. Metress. "Depression." in **Aging and Health: Biologic and Social Perspectives,** by Cary S. Kart, Eileen S. Metress and James F. Metress, 185-186. Menlo Park, CA: Addison-Wesley, 1978.

Drugs for depression and other conditions are frequently prescribed for the elderly because health care practitioners are impatient, when dealing with these patients.

3.054. Kavanagh, Terence. "Depression Following Heart Attack." in **Take Heart!: A Proven Step-by-Step Program to Improve Your Heart's Health,** by Terence Kavanagh, 293-295. Toronto, ON: Key Porter Books, 1992.

A depressed heart patient can benefit greatly from an exercise program. Fitness enhances self-confidence and improves morale. These patients are apprehensive about exertion and question the value of an exercise program. They look for excuses to drop out of the program. These patients need encouragement and reassurance.

3.055. Klein, Donald F. "Agitated Depression." in **Drug Treatment of Mental Disorders,** edited by Lance L. Simpson, 70-71. New York, NY: Raven, 1976.

3.056. Klerman, Gerald L. "Psychopharmacologic Treatment of Depression." Chapter in **Clinical Psychopharmacology,** edited by Jerrold G. Bernstein, 63-79. Littleton, MA: PSG Publishing, 1978.

3.057. Klinger, Eric. "Worried Daydreams that Persist: Grief and Depression." in **Daydreaming: Using Waking Fantasy and Imagery for Self-Knowledge and Creativity,** by Eric Klinger, 270-272. Los Angeles, CA: Jeremy P. Tarcher, 1990.

3.058. Korb, Kathy L., Stacey D. Azok and Estelle A. Leutenberg. "Depressed? Feeling Blue? What Can I Do?" in **Life Management Skills II: Reproducible Activity Handouts Created for Facilitators,** by Kathy L. Korb, Stacey D. Azok and Estelle A. Leutenberg, 16. Beachwood, OH: Wellness Reproductions, 1991.

There are in this sample handout eighteen things a depressed person can do to cope with depression.

3.059. Lazarus, Arnold. "The Role of Imagery in Overcoming Sadness and Despondency." Chapter in **In the Mind's Eye: The Power of Imagery for Personal Enrichment,** by Arnold Lazarus, 127-145. New York, NY: Rawson Associates, 1977.

Imagery brings about optimism and pessimism. The person who focuses on positive imagery anticipates positive events and takes action to experience these events. Pessimistic imagery leads to negative experiences. When a person experiences positive imagery and negative imagery intrudes, this person should immediately focus back to positive imagery. The severity of depression will increase when a person dwells on his losses or liabilities and decrease when a person focuses on his gains or assets.

3.060. Levy, Bernard. "Lithium Treatment of Atypical Manic-Depressive Illness." Chapter in **Clinical Psychopharmacology,** edited by Jerrold G. Bernstein, 80-85. Littleton, MA: PSG Publishing, 1978.

3.061. Lewinsohn, Peter M., Anthony Biglan and Antonette M. Zeiss. "Behavioral Treatment of Depression." Chapter in **The Behavioral Management of Anxiety, Depression and Pain,** edited by Park O. Davidson, 91-146. New York, NY: Brunner/Mazel, 1976.

This and the other four papers in this book are based on papers presented at the 1975 Banff International Conference on Behavior Modification.

3.062. Lewinsohn, Peter M., Julia Steinmetz Breckenridge, David O. Antonuccio and Linda Teri. "A Behavioral Group Therapy Approach to the Treatment of Depression." Chapter in **Handbook of Behavioral Group Therapy,** edited by Dennis Upper and Steven M. Ross, 303-329. New York, NY: Plenum, 1985.

Coping with Depression (CWD) is a course offered through the University of Oregon Depression Research Unit. This course has been since 1979 offered to more than 300 depressed persons. There is in course participants significant improvement in depression level and in diagnosis. The CWD allows outreach and is readily accessible to a variety of depressed individuals. Author biographical information. 3 tables. 110 references.

3.063. Macleod, John. "Major Depressive Illness." in **Davidson's Principles and Practice of Medicine: A Textbook for Students and Doctors,** Fourteenth Edition, edited by John Macleod, 681-682. Edinburgh: Churchill Livingstone, 1984.

Patients on monoamine oxidase inhibitors (MAOIs) should be informed of precautionary measures to take regarding these drugs. Patients should not eat cheese and should not drink Chianti because the cheese and wine both contain tyramine. The tyramine and drugs may interact to precipitate a hypertensive crisis. Patients should also avoid other drugs, Pethidine being one example. There should be a one-week, drug-free interval between the time patients change from using MAOIs to the time they begin using tricyclics, and vice versa.

3.064. Mayerson, Evelyn Wilde. "Uncovering Depression." in **Putting the Ill at Ease,** by Evelyn Wilde Mayerson, 259-260. Hagerstown, MD: Harper and Row, 1976.

Involvement with something new - even for aged patients - is an excellant deterrent to depression. These individuals must be convinced change is possible. The aged can learn, even if they learn at a slower rate than other age groups.

3.065. McGee, Mark G. and David W. Wilson. "Antidepressants." in **Psychology: Science and Application,** by Mark G. McGee and David W. Wilson, 436. St. Paul, MN: West Publishing, 1984.

3.066. McGee, Mark G. and David W. Wilson. "Antimanics." in **Psychology: Science and Application,** by Mark G. McGee and David W. Wilson, 436-437. St. Paul, MN: West Publishing, 1984.

Lithium carbonate is the only known effective drug used to treat the mania in bipolar disorder.

3.067. McGee, Mark G. and David W. Wilson. "Electroconvulsive Therapy." in **Psychology: Science and Application**, by Mark G. McGee and David W. Wilson, 437-438. St. Paul, MN: West Publishing, 1984.

When electroconvulsive therapy (ECT), also known as electroshock, is used to treat depression, an electric current of seventy to 130 volts passes through the brain. After the Northern California Psychiatric Society challenged the legality of the ban in 1982 on ECT use in Berkeley, California the ban was terminated. This illustrates the controversy this treatment can cause. When ECT is restricted to one side of the brain, the likelihood of memory impairment is lessened considerably. ECT is the treatment option when other methods are not effective against severe depression. 1 photograph.

3.068. McGee, Mark G. and David W. Wilson. "Psychosurgery." in **Psychology: Science and Application**, by Mark G. McGee and David W. Wilson, 438. St. Paul, MN: West Publishing, 1984.

Psychosurgery is brain surgery which alleviates, for example, depression. Lobotomy exemplifies this type of surgery. A lobotomy can also be performed to control violent behavior. After drug therapies were extensively used in the 1950s, interest in lobotimies decreased. Present-day psychosurgery is sophisticated, precise, and involves small areas of the brain. Jack Nicholson played the role of a person who, in the movie **One Flew over the Cuckoo's Nest**, had a lobotomy. 1 photograph.

3.069. McHugh, Paul R. "Manic-Depressive Psychosis." in **Cecil Textbook of Medicine**, Volume Two, Seventeenth Edition, edited by James B. Wyngaarden and Lloyd H. Smith, Jr., 2005-2007. Philadelphia, PA: W.B. Saunders, 1985.

Manic-depressive attacks appear more frequently in spring and fall. Drugs relieve symptoms of depression. Electroconvulsive treatment (ECT) terminates depression, usually after four to eight sessions. Recovery can be dramatic and quick. Patients usually recover completely, even without treatment, in approximately six months. After a person has had one episode of affective disturbance, it may be many years before another episode occurs. 5 references.

3.070. McLean, Peter. "Therapeutic Decision-Making in the Behavioral Treatment of Depression." Chapter in **The Behavioral Management of Anxiety, Depression and Pain**, edited by Park O. Davidson, 54-90. New York, NY: Brunner/Mazel, 1976.

3.071. Meares, Ainslie. "Depression." in **A System of Medical Hypnosis**, by Ainslie Meares, 292-294. Philadelphia, PA: W.B. Saunders, 1960.

Electroconvulsive therapy (ECT) and antidepressants - not hypnosis - are recommended for the treatment of simple endogenous depression and agitated melancholia. Suggestive hypnosis is recommended for the treatment of reactive depressive states.

3.072. Mendelson, Jack H. and Nancy K. Mello. "Alcohol and Depression." in **Alcohol: Use and Abuse in America**, by Jack H. Mendelson and Nancy K. Mello, 203-204. Boston, MA: Little, Brown and Company, 1985.

Alcohol was administered intravenously to psychiatric patients afflicted with a depressive disorder. The alcohol, according to these patients, did not appear to have any significant effect on them. They felt relatively the same before and after they were administered the alcohol. Alcohol is not an effective antidepressant in view of the close relationship between suicide and alcohol intoxication.

3.073. Mendelson, Jack H. and Nancy K. Mello. "Antidepressants." in **Alcohol: Use and Abuse in America**, by Jack H. Mendelson and Nancy K. Mello, 296-297. Boston, MA: Little, Brown and Company, 1985.

Lithium was first used in the middle 1800s to treat gout. The monoamine oxidase inhibitors (MOAIs) were first developed to treat tuberculosis. The precursor of the tricyclic antidepressants was used unsuccessfully as an antihistamine. Each of these three classes of drugs was subsequently used to treat depressive illness.

3.074. Mendelson, Jack H. and Nancy K. Mello. "Depression and Alcoholism." in **Alcohol: Use and Abuse in America**, by Jack H. Mendelson and Nancy K. Mello, 238-240. Boston, MA: Little, Brown and Company, 1985.

3.075. Murphy, Dennis L. "Neuropharmacology of Depression." Chapter in **Drug Treatment of Mental Disorders**, edited by Lance L. Simpson, 109-125. New York, NY: Raven, 1976.

3.076. Neuman, R. Emil. "Depression (The Blues)." in **The Complete Handbook of Health Tips: Based on the Latest Nutritional and Scientific Findings and Time-Proven Remedies**, by R. Emil Neuman, 63-65, N.p., United Research Publishers, 1985.

Calcium, magnesium, folic acid, tyrosine, tryptophane, vitamin B-6, and phenylalanine are helpful in treating depression.

3.077. Olson, Ken. "A Physical Basis for Depression." in **Can You Wait Till Friday?: The Psychology of Hope,** by Ken Olson, 150. Greenwich, CT: Fawcett, 1975.

Lithium, although not without its side effects, is effective against certain types of depression.

3.078. Pantano, James A. "Postoperative Depression." in **Living with Angina: A Practical Guide to Dealing with Coronary Artery Disease and Your Doctor,** by James A. Pantano, 155-156. New York, NY: HarperPerennial, 1990.

Postoperative depression in coronary patients relates to issues of immortality, advancement at work, travel, job stress, and other personal, work, and economic matters.

3.079. Papalia, Diane E. and Sally Wendkos Olds. "Bipolar Disorder ("Manic-Depression")." in **Psychology,** by Diane E. Papalia and Sally Wendkos Olds, 572. New York, NY: McGraw-Hill, 1985.

Lithium carbonate controls manic states, often eliminating symptoms entirely. This drug, although not habit forming, can negatively affect the thyroid gland and kidneys. It can also cause weight gain.

3.080. Papalia, Diane E. and Sally Wendkos Olds. "Depression." in **Psychology,** by Diane E. Papalia and Sally Wendkos Olds, 572. New York, NY: McGraw-Hill, 1985.

The tricyclics and monoamine oxidase (MAO) inhibitors are used to treat depression. Both classes of drugs were developed in the 1950s. Elavil, Sinequan, and Aventyl are examples of the most common tricyclics. Marplan, Nardil, and Parnate are examples of MAO inhibitors. These and other antidepressants may take a week or longer to take effect. Electric shock therapy may have to be administered to the suicidal person until antidepressant medication begins to work.

3.081. Peachey, John. "Drug Treatment of Affective Disorders." in **The International Handbook of Addiction Behaviour,** edited by Ilana Belle Glass, 212-214. London: Tavistock/Routledge, 1991.

3.082. Raskind, Murray and Carl Eisdorfer. "Antidepressant Drugs." in **Drug Treatment of Mental Disorders,** edited by Lance L. Simpson, 245-250. New York, NY: Raven, 1976.

3.083. Rathus, Spencer A. and Jeffrey S. Nevid. "Coping with Depression." in **Psychology and the Challenges of Life: Adjustment and Growth,** by Spencer A. Rathus and Jeffrey S. Nevid, 379-386. New York, NY: Holt, Rinehart and Winston, 1989.

The Pleasant Events Schedule - A List of Turn-Ons is a list of 116 things many people enjoy. The list can be used to enhance the quality of a person's life. A person places a 0 "not pleasant," 1 "pleasant," or 2 "very pleasant" beside each of the 116 activities/events. The list helps indicate things a person can choose to do to have a more meaningful daily life. 2 tables. The second table, Table 10.8, is a list of ten irrational, depressing thoughts, and rational alternatives to these thoughts. 1 photograph.

3.084. Reid, William H. "Mood Disorders." Chapter in **The Treatment of Psychiatric Disorders: Revised for the DSM-III-R,** by William H. Reid, 204-244. New York, NY: Brunner/Mazel, 1989.

3.085. Rogers, Malcolm P. and Patricia L. McGuire. "Management of Depression." Chapter in **Office Practice of Medicine,** Second Edition, by William T. Branch, Jr., 1307-1323. Philadelphia, PA: W.B. Saunders, 1987.

3.086. Root, Maria P.P., Patricia Fallon and William N. Friedrich. "Bulimia as an Affective Disorder." in **Bulimia: A Systems Approach to Treatment,** by Maria P.P. Root, Patricia Fallon and William N. Friedrich, 208-210. New York, NY: W.W. Norton and Company, 1986.

When a group of bulimics was administered a monoamine oxidase inhibitor (MAOI), both depression and bulimic symptoms were reduced. Cognitive patterns of thinking, repressed anger, physiological starvation, and powerlessness within the social system are the probable causes of depression and mood variations in bulimics.

3.087. Rudestam, Kjell Erik. "Depression." in **Methods of Self-Change: An ABC Primer,** by Kjell Erik Rudestam, 211-221. Monterey, CA: Brooks/Cole, 1980.

A depressed person in Japan may undergo a type of therapy called Morita therapy. This is a type of psychotherapy. The patient remains in bed for a week and does not receive usual sources of reinforcement. The depressed person then has to do physical work. Stimuli which used to be rewarding and meaningful tend to be experienced by the patient as once again rewarding and meaningful. 1 photograph.

3.088. Sgroi, Suzanne M. and Natalie T. Dana. "Depression." in **Handbook of Clinical Intervention in Child Sexual Abuse,** by Suzanne M. Sgroi, 197. Lexington, MA: Lexington Books, 1982.

3.089. Shames, Richard and Karilee Halo Shames. "Escaping the Grip of Depression." Chapter in **The Gift of Health: A Holistic Approach to Higher-Quality, Lower-Cost Health Care,** by Richard Shames and Karilee Halo Shames, 78-89. New York, NY: Bantam Books, 1982.

Diet, deep breathing, and exercise can help a person overcome depression.

3.090. Shipley, Kenneth. "Avoid Displaying Anxiety about the Griever's Depression." in **Interviewing and Counseling in Communicative Disorders: Principles and Procedures,** by Kenneth Shipley, 206-207. New York, NY: Macmillan, 1992.

3.091. Silverman, Robert E. "Cognitive Therapy in the Treatment of Depression." in **Psychology,** Fourth Edition, by Robert E. Silverman, 494. Englewood Cliffs, NJ: Prentice-Hall, 1982.

3.092. Simon, Gregory E. "Management of Depression." in **Outpatient Medicine,** edited by Stephan D. Fihn and Steven R. McGee, 601-605. Philadelphia, PA: W.B. Saunders, 1992.

3.093. Snyder, Solomon H. "Understanding and Treating Depression." Chapter in **The Troubled Mind: A Guide to Release from Distress,** by Solomon H. Snyder, 71-85. New York, NY: McGraw-Hill, 1976.

Dr. John Cade, an Australian psychiatrist, discovered lithium in 1949. Dr. Mogens Schou has experimented in Sweden, since the 1950s, with lithium in the treatment of mania and depression. Lithium is a commonly occurring metal which stabilizes patients without sedating them.

3.094. Trembley, Edward L. "Understanding and Alleviating Depression." in **Helping Clients with Special Concerns**, by Sheldon Eisenberg and Lewis E. Patterson, 55-78. Chicago, IL: Rand McNally, 1979.

3.095. Vickery, Donald M. and James F. Fries. "Depression." in **Take Care of Yourself: Your Personal Guide to Self-Care and Preventing Illness**, Fourth Edition, 420-421. Reading, MA: Addison Wesley, 1989.

Regular exercise can be just as effective in alleviating mild depression as can doctor-prescribed drugs.

3.096. Wadeson, Harriet. "Combining Expressive Therapies in an Effort to Survive on a Depression Ward." Chapter in **Art Psychotherapy**, by Harriet Wadeson, 102-110. New York, NY: John Wiley and Sons, 1980.

3.097. Wadeson, Harriet. "Comparison of Art Expression in Schizophrenia, Depression, and Manic-Depressive Psychosis." Chapter in **Art Psychotherapy**, by Harriet Wadeson, 188-198. New York, NY: John Wiley and Sons, 1980.

3.098. Watson, David L. and Roland G. Tharp. "Depression and Low Self-Esteem." in **Self-Directed Behavior: Self-Modification for Personal Adjustment**, Fifth Edition, by David L. Watson and Roland G. Tharp, 87. Pacific Grove, CA: Brooks/Cole, 1989.

Depressed individuals can understand their depressions better - can get a more complete, realistic idea of them - by noting positive events in their lives. They can begin by monitoring their moods four times daily. Only rarely is a day all bad. It is for this reason depressed persons will probably see more fluctuations in their moods than they would have expected.

3.099. Watson, David L. and Roland G. Tharp. "Depression and Low Self-Esteem." in **Self-Directed Behavior: Self-Modification for Personal Adjustment**, Fifth Edition, by David L. Watson and Roland G. Tharp, 143-144. Pacific Grove, CA: Brooks/Cole, 1989.

A new environment, one in which social interactions can be rewarded more readily, is perhaps the single most effective way to overcome depression. This will often heighten mood and self-esteem. Depressed persons should try to have more realistic goals and standards. Positive self-statements can be used immediately after disappointments. This is because depressed individuals negatively overgeneralize after disappointments.

3.100. Watson, David L. and Roland G. Tharp. "Depression and Low Self-Esteem." in **Self-Directed Behavior: Self-Modification for Personal Adjustment,** Fifth Edition, by David L. Watson and Roland G. Tharp, 227-228. Pacific Grove, CA: Brooks/Cole, 1989.

The depressed individual is probably not receiving from other people enough reinforcement. It will likely be necessary to acquire new habits to correct this matter. Social-skill building will contribute to solving the problem.

3.101. Watson, David L. and Roland G. Tharp. "Specific New Behaviors." in **Self-Directed Behavior: Self-Modification for Personal Adjustment,** Fifth Edition, by David L. Watson and Roland G. Tharp, 183-184. Pacific Grove, CA: Brooks/Cole, 1989.

Pleasant activities, including small pleasures, will fight depression. These activities can be extremely diverse. Telephoning a friend, sewing, and gardening are examples. Regular exercise - aerobic and nonaerobic - lowers depression.

3.102. Welch, Charles A. "Electroconvulsive Therapy in the General Hospital." Chapter in **Massachusetts General Hospital Handbook of General Hospital Psychiatry,** Third Edition, edited by Ned H. Cassem, 269-280. St. Louis, MO: Mosby Year Book, 1991.

Many depressed patients are not responsive to drugs or are responsive, but drug side effects are excessively adverse. This is the reason electroconvulsive therapy (ECT) is a viable treatment option for certain depressed persons. Although drug treatment is the first line of therapy for mania, mania responds well to ECT. Depressed patients, and those with Parkinson's disease, both improve after ECT. Cardiac arrest is rarely associated with ECT and 0.03% is the mortality rate for ECT patients. Stress to the heart and brain is the most important physiological stress during ECT. **The Practice of Electroconvulsive Therapy: Recommendations, Training, and Privileging,** published in 1990 by the American Psychiatric Association Task Force, contains very rigorous practice guidelines. 71 references.

3.103. Wender, Paul H. and Donald F. Klein. "Antidepressants." in **Mind, Mood, and Medicine: A Guide to the New**

Biopsychiatry, by Paul H. Wender and Donald F. Klein, 150-152. New York, NY: Farrar • Straus - Giroux, 1981.

A Swiss pharmaceutical firm created, in the mid-1950s, Tofranil (imipramine). Roland Kuhn, a German psychiatrist, administered imipramine to psychiatric patients, in whom depression was the predominant symptom. He noted this drug was effective in treating severe depression.

3.104. Wender, Paul H. and Donald F. Klein. "Lithium." in **Mind, Mood, and Medicine: A Guide to the New Biopsychiatry,** by Paul H. Wender and Donald F. Klein, 152-153. New York, NY: Farrar • Straus - Giroux, 1981.

3.105. Wender, Paul H. and Donald F. Klein. "Lithium." in **Mind, Mood, and Medicine: A Guide to the New Biopsychiatry,** by Paul H. Wender and Donald F. Klein, 346-349. New York, NY: Farrar • Straus - Giroux, 1981.

Increased frequency of urination, mild thirst, mild nausea, and loose stools are associated with some patients, during initial lithium treatment. Hypothyroidism can result in some patients. Dosage for each patient must be individual-specific and, initially, a blood test must be taken each time the dosage is increased. Lithium, however, is non-habit-forming.

3.106. Wender, Paul H. and Donald F. Klein. "Major Tranquilizers." in **Mind, Mood, and Medicine: A Guide to the New Biopsychiatry,** by Paul H. Wender and Donald F. Klein, 349-351. New York, NY: Farrar • Straus - Giroux, 1981.

Chlorpromazine (Thorazine), trifluoperazine (Stelazine), and thiothixene (Havane) are a few examples of major tranquilizers. A skin rash and severe sore throat will indicate an allergic reaction to these tranquilzers. Muscular stiffness and trembling will appear in some patients. The neurological disorder tardive dyskinesia will appear in certain patients taking large doses for many years. Physician monitoring of tranquilizers is imperative.

3.107. Wender, Paul H. and Donald F. Klein. "Minor Tranquilizers." in **Mind, Mood, and Medicine: A Guide to the New Biopsychiatry,** by Paul H. Wender and Donald F. Klein, 351-352. New York, NY: Farrar • Straus - Giroux, 1981.

The benzodiazepines are the most effective minor tranquilizers. Librium, Valium, and Tranxene are common examples.

Drowsiness is a typical side effect when the drugs are first taken. Driving a car at this time should be avoided. These drugs, furthermore, accentuate the effects of alcohol.

3.108. Williams, Robert L. and James D. Long. "Depression." in **Toward a Self-Managed Life Style**, by Robert L. Williams and James D. Long, 163-165. Boston, MA: Houghton Mifflin, 1975.

Positive self-verbalization is a strategy used to enhance mood and self-esteem. This strategy allays depression when the positive aspects of a person's life are emphasized.

3.109. Wolff, Anthony. "Medicine for Melancholy." in **Mind and Supermind: A Saturday Review Report**, edited by Albert Rosenfeld, 237-245. New York, NY: Holt, Rinehart and Winston, 1977.

Drs. Ronald R. Fieve and Nathan S. Kline are proponents of the chemical treatment of depression. They feel traditional psychotherapy will play a relatively minor role in the treatment of depression and other psychiatric disorders. Emotional symptoms, according to these two doctors, do not necessarily have an emotional cause. There are physical, metabolic, and chemical causes of depression. Past problems in a person's life do not cause moodswing. Dr. Fieve uses lithium to control manic depression.

3.110. Zastrow, Charles. "How to Handle Being Depressed." Chapter in **The Personal Problem Solver**, edited by Charles Zastrow and Dae H. Chang, 29-34. Englewood Cliffs, NJ: Prentice-Hall, 1977.

Meaningful activity; rational-emotive therapy; and antidepressant drugs, such as imipramine and lithium, can be helpful in the management of mild depression.

3.111. Zimbardo, Philip G. "Antidepressant Drugs." in **Psychology and Life**, Twelfth Edition, by Philip G. Zimbardo, 589-590. Glenview, IL: Scott, Foresman and Company, 1988.

3.112. Zimbardo, Philip G. "Cognitive Therapy for Depression." in **Psychology and Life**, Twelfth Edition, by Philip G. Zimbardo, 580. Glenview, IL: Scott, Foresman and Company, 1988.

Aaron Beck has applied cognitive therapy for the treatment of depression.

GOVERNMENT DOCUMENTS AND ASSOCIATION PUBLICATIONS

3.113. American Psychiatric Association. **Treatments of Psychiatric Disorders: A Task Force Report of the American Psychiatric Association,** Volume Three. Washington, DC: American Psychiatric Association, 1989.

A variety of treatment options are available for the treatment of mood disorders including: (1) electroconvulsive therapy (ECT), (2) psychoanalysis, (3) light therapy, (4) psychosurgery, and (5) antidepressants.

3.114. Rounsaville, Bruce J., Thomas R. Kosten, Myrna M. Weissman and Herbert D. Kleber. **Evaluating and Treating Depressive Disorders in Opiate Addicts.** Rockville, MD: National Institute on Drug Abuse, 1985. DHHS Publication No. (ADM) 85-1406.

CONFERENCES, MEETINGS, SEMINARS, SYMPOSIA, AND WORKSHOPS

3.115. Fann, William E., Ismet Karacan, Alex D. Pokorny and Robert L. Williams. Editors. **Phenomenology and Treatment of Depression.** New York, NY: Spectrum, 1977.

A publication of twenty-two chapters by thirty contributors resulted from a symposium held in Houston, Texas, December 4-5, 1975. The Department of Psychiatry and the Office of Continuing Education of Baylor College of Medicine sponsored the symposium. Ten pharmaceutical manufacturers provided financial support. Adolescent eating disorders, sleep, and suicide, in relation to depression, were each discussed in three separate chapters, in addition to nineteen other topics.

PARTS OF CONFERENCES, MEETINGS, SEMINARS, SYMPOSIA, AND WORKSHOPS

3.116. Fine, Eric W. "The Syndrome of Alcohol Dependency and Depression." Chapter in **Substance Abuse and Psychiatric Illness: Proceedings of the Second Annual Coatesville-Jefferson Conference on Addiction,** edited by Edward Gottheil, A. Thomas McLellan and Keith A. Druley, 134-139. New York, NY: Pergamon, 1980.

REVIEW PAPERS

3.117. Ananth, J. and D. Luchins. "A Review of Combined Tricyclic and MAOI Therapy." **Comprehensive Psychiatry** 18 (May-June 1977): 221-230.

Combined tricyclic and MAOI (monoamine oxidase inhibitor) therapy, if properly administered, does not lead to serious complications, nor to excessive minor side effects. Author biographical information. 4 tables. 47 references.

3.118. Asnis, Gregory. "Parkinson's Disease, Depression, and ECT: A Review and Case Study." **American Journal of Psychiatry** 134 (February 1977): 191-195.

Depression may be reactive and biochemically related to Parkinson's disease. A sixty-one-year-old male, experiencing psychotic depression and parkinsonism, responded positively to ECT (electroconvulsive therapy). A depression rating scale confirmed the improvement. Author biographical information. Abstract. Acknowledgements. 3 figures. 29 references.

3.119. Birley, J.L.T. "Modified Frontal Leucotomy: A Review of 106 Cases." **British Journal of Psychiatry** 110 (March 1964): 211-221.

The subjects in this research were 106 patients referred to Dr. W. Sargant at St. Thomas's Hospital. These patients had, between 1950 and 1957, a bilateral frontal leucotomy. Prefrontal leucotomy, on follow-up, appears to considerably benefit certain psychiatric patients. Author biographical information. 9 tables. Acknowledgements. 30 references.

3.120. Brumback, Roger A., Susan G. Dietz-Schmidt and Warren A. Weinberg. "Depression in Children Referred to an Educational Diagnostic Center: Diagnosis and Treatment and Analysis of Criteria and Literature Review." **Diseases of the Nervous System** 38 (July 1977): 529-535.

Some of the findings: (1) eighty-nine percent of depressed children were from families in which there was affective disorder; (2) depressed children exhibited hyperactivity, temper tantrums and school phobia significantly more frequently than did nondepressed children; and (3) ninety-five percent of depressed children improved clinically after they were treated with antidepressants. Author biographical information. 10 tables. 23 references. Acknowledgement. 1 figure.

3.121. Cole, Jonathan O. "Therapeutic Efficacy of Antidepressant Drugs." **Journal of the American Medical Association** 190 (November 2, 1964): 448-455.

Although Tofranil, Elavil, and Parnate are more effective in treating depression than is a placebo, none of these drugs appear to be more effective than ECT (electroconvulsive therapy) in treating severe depression. The monoamine oxidase inhibitors (MAOIs) are less desirable as initial treatment because they have greater potential for alarming reactions with other agents. Author biographical information. 72 references.

3.122. Conte, Hope R. and T. Byram Karasu. "A Review of Treatment Studies of Minor Depression: 1980-1991." **American Journal of Psychotherapy** 46 (January 1992): 58-74.

3.123. "Diagnosis and Treatment of Depression in Late Life: Summary of the NIH Consensus Statement." **Maryland Medical Journal** 42 (February 1993): 192-194.

3.124. Hurwitz, Thomas D. "Electroconvulsive Therapy: A Review." **Comprehensive Psychiatry** 15 (July-August 1974): 303-314.

Electroconvulsive therapy (ECT) is a safe, effective, and easy-to-use method of treating depression, mania, and schizophrenia. Author biographical information. 5 tables. 54 references.

3.125. Jefferson, James W. "A Review of the Cardiovascular Effects and Toxicity of Tricyclic Antidepressants." **Psychosomatic Medicine** 37 (March-April 1975): 160-179.

Although tricyclic antidepressants can cause, in part, arrhythmias and congestive heart failure, these changes occur most commonly with overdose, not at therapeutic levels. There can occur, furthermore, interactions between the tricyclics and cardiovascular disease treatment agents. Author biographical information. Abstract. 3 tables. 147 references.

3.126. Kearney, Christopher A. "Depression and School Refusal Behavior: A Review with Comments on Classification and Treatment." **Journal of School Psychology** 31 (Summer 1993): 267-279.

3.127. Morris, Jeffery B. and Aaron T. Beck. "The Efficacy of Antidepressant Drugs: A Review of Research (1958-1972)." **Archives of General Psychiatry** 30 (May 1974): 667-674.

3.128. Quitkin, Frederic, Arthur Rifkin and Donald F. Klein. "Monoamine Oxidase Inhibitors: A Review of Antidepressant Effectiveness." **Archvies of General Psychiatry** 36 (July 1979): 749-760.

3.129. Robertson, Mary M. and M.R. Trimble. "Major Tranquillisers Used as Antidepressants: A Review." **Journal of Affective Disorders** 4 (September 1982): 173-193.

3.130. Sachar, Edward J. "Corticosteroids in Depressive Illness. I. A Reevaluation of Control Issues and the Literature." **Archives of General Psychiatry** 17 (November 1967): 544-553.

3.131. Shearer, Steven L. and Gillian Kaplin Adams. "Nonpharmacologic Aids in the Treatment of Depression." **American Family Physician** 47 (February 1, 1993): 435-443.

Self-help materials on depression, which can be used by patients and their families, is one nonpharmacologic option in the treatment of depression. Cognitive therapy, and its emphasis on correcting cognitive distortions in depressed persons, is another nonpharmacologic option. Many irrational beliefs contribute to depression. One belief is that a person should be loved by virtually everyone in the community. Another belief is that the world should be a just place. Author biographical information. Abstract. 4 tables. 13 references. Two-page patient information handout on depression.

3.132. Siris, Samuel G., Daniel P. van Kammen and John P. Docherty. "Use of Antidepressant Drugs in Schizophrenia." **Archives of General Psychiatry** 35 (November 1978): 1368-1377.

Examples of findings: (1) the use of tricyclic antidepressants and monoamine oxidase inhibitors (MAOIs) was not warranted in schizophrenia, except in the pseudoneurotic subgroup; (2) combinations of antidepressants and phenothiazines were not, in most cases, more beneficial than phenothiazines alone; and (3) nonanergic clinically depressed patients often benefited by use of tricyclic antidepressants and MAOIs. Author biographical information. Abstract. 4 tables. 175 references.

3.133. Trimble, Michael. "Non-Monoamine Oxidase Inhibitor Antidepressants and Epilepsy: A Review." **Epilepsia** 19 (June 1978): 241-250.

Imipramine was the first tricyclic antidepressant to be used clinically. This drug was introduced in 1958, after research in Switzerland. There were initially minor side effects. Major side effects, including epileptic seizures, were noted after increased use of imipramine. There were seizures in patients who were administered normal doses and in patients who took an overdose. Amitriptyline was introduced next. Author biographical information. 71 references. French abstract. Spanish abstract. German abstract.

3.134. Walter, C.J.S., Nita Mitchell-Heggs and William Sargant. "Modified Narcosis, ECT and Antidepressant Drugs: A Review of Technique and Immediate Outcome." **British Journal of Psychiatry** 120 (June 1972): 651-662.

Some of the results after combined treatment: (1) patients with severe obsessional neuroses - 43%, symptom-free or much improved; (2) patients with long-standing schizophrenia or schizo-affective states - 41%, symptom-free or much improved; and (3) patients with chronic anxiety - 55%, recovered or improved markedly. Author biographical information. 5 tables. Acknowledgements. 21 references.

3.135. Will, Otto Allen, Jr., Frederick Cooper Rehfeldt and Meta A. Neumann. "A Fatality in Electroshock Therapy: Report of a Case and Review of Certain Previously Described Cases." **Journal of Nervous and Mental Disease** 107 (February 1948): 105-126.

Among the highlights: (1) thirty-three fatalities occurred after electroshock therapy (ECT); (2) over forty was the age of the majority of patients; (3) at least sixteen patients had received fewer than nine ECTs before death; and (4) twenty-six of thirty-three deaths were apparently related to ECT. Author biographical information. 115 references.

Chapter 4

PROZAC (FLUOXETINE)

BOOKS FOR PROFESSIONALS AND THE GENERAL PUBLIC

4.001. Breggin, Peter R. and Ginger Ross Breggin. **Talking Back to Prozac: What Doctors Won't Tell You about Today's Most Controversial Drug.** New York, NY: St. Martin's Press, 1994.

4.002. Fieve, Ronald R. **Prozac: Questions and Answers for Patients, Family, and Physicians.** New York, NY: Avon Books, 1994.

Over 200 questions and answers are provided regarding prozac in relation to side effects, aggression, suicide, personality, and genetics.

4.003. Kramer, Peter D. **Listening to Prozac: A Psychiatrist Explores Antidepressant Drugs and the Remaking of the Self.** New York, NY: Viking, 1993.

CHAPTERS AND SECTIONS IN BOOKS FOR PROFESSIONALS AND THE GENERAL PUBLIC

4.004. Alexopoulos, George S. "Fluoxetine." in **Clinical Geriatric Psychopharmacology,** Second Edition, edited by Carl Salzman, 148-149. Baltimore, MD: Williams and Wilkins, 1992.

Two to three days is the elimination half-life for fluoxetine, longer than that of any other antidepressant. Fluoxetine metabolizes in the liver to form norfluoxetine. Fluoxetine, for this reason, takes about one week to reach steady blood levels. Fluoxetine has fewer side effects in geriatric patients than do amitriptyline and doxepin, while appearing to be as effective as these two drugs.

4.005. Baldwin, Robert C. "Table 19.1: Comparison of the Effects of Different Antidepressants." in **Psychiatry in the Elderly,** edited by Robin Jacoby and Catherine Oppenheimer, 697. Oxford: Oxford University Press, 1991.

The effects of ten different antidepressants, including fluoxetine, are compared in terms of main amine effect, anticholinergic effect, orthostatic effect, sedation, and initial dose in mg.

4.006. Cleghorn, John M. and Betty Lou Lee. "Depression." Chapter in **Understanding and Treating Mental Illness: The Strengths and Limits of Modern Psychiatry**, by John M. Cleghorn and Betty Lou Lee, 55-78. Toronto, ON: Hogrefe and Huber, 1991.

Tables and figures - most of them reproduced from the **British Journal of Psychiatry** (1988), Supplement 3 - provide a variety of data about fluoxetine: (1) "Table 3.1: Frequency of Adverse Reactions - Antidepressants;" (2) "Table 3.2: Summary Quote from **British Journal of Psychiatry** 1988;" (3) "Figure 3.1: The Most Common Adverse Events Associated with Discontinuation in Comparative Clinical Trials;" (4) "Figure 3.2: The Most Common Adverse Events with Fluoxetine in Comparative Clinical Trials;" and (5) "Figure 3.3: Adverse Events in Geriatric Patients vs All Patients Treated with Fluoxetine." There is also "Table 3.3: Excerpt from Physician Pamphlet Regarding Clinical Pharmacology of Prozac." 3 tables. 8 figures. 4 associations. 5 books.

4.007. Dagon, Eugene M. and Ashok Raj. "Fluoxetine (Prozac)." in **Clinical Geriatric Neurology**, edited by Laurie Barclay, 376. Philadelphia, PA: Lea and Febiger, 1993.

Fluoxetine, when compared with doxepin, causes a decrease in heart rate, but not in blood pressure. Even after several months, fluoxetine does not accumulate - in spite of its long half-life - in the blood of elderly patients.

4.008. "Fluoxetine." in **Complete Drug Reference 1994 Edition**, 652-654. Yonkers, NY: Consumers Union, 1993.

Patients who are prescribed fluoxetine should discuss this drug with their physician before taking it because there have been allegations that, in a few patients, fluoxetine increased in these patients thoughts about suicide.

4.009. "Fluoxetine Hydrochloride." in **Nursing Student's Guide to Drugs**, 434-436. Springhouse, PA: Springhouse, 1993.

Fluoxetine should not be administered to individuals who have taken MAO (monoamine oxidase) inhibitors within fourteen days of starting the administration of fluoxetine. This drug should be used cautiously in underweight persons because fluoxetine may bring about significant weight loss. If a patient develops a rash while on fluoxetine, fluoxetine should be discontinued. Insomnia may be prevented by not administering this medication in the evening.

4.010. "Fluoxetine Hydrochloride." in **The Pill Book**, Sixth Edition, 394-398. New York, NY: Bantam Books, 1994.

Prozac is the brand name of the antidepressant drug whose generic name is fluoxetine hydrochloride. Prozac has also been used in treating bulimia and obsessive-compulsive disorders. This drug can improve mood and sleep patterns and can increase a person's physical activity. No unusual adverse effects have been reported in senior citizens using this medication. Abnormal dreams, acne, twitching, and anemia are some of Prozac's less common side effects.

4.011. Frenkel, Abraham R., Frederic M. Quitkin and Judith G. Rabkin. "Fluoxetine." in **Adverse Effects of Psychotropic Drugs**, edited by John M. Kane and Jeffrey A. Lieberman, 121-123. New York, NY: Guilford Press, 1992.

M.H. Teicher, C. Glod, and J.O. Cole attributed in an article in 1990, on the basis of six patients, suicidal ideation to fluoxetine. Some of their patients suffered from temporal lobe epilepsy, others from paranoia. Most of the patients were also on other medication. Suicidal ideation, common in depression, has been associated with all types of antidepressants. Anecdotal reports are not synonymous with statistically significant information. The article by Teicher, Glod, and Cole is viewed as anecdotal.

4.012. Glassman, Alexander H. and Gregory W. Dalack. "Fluoxetine." in **Adverse Effects of Psychotropic Drugs**, edited by John M. Kane and Jeffrey A. Lieberman, 294-295. New York, NY: Guilford Press, 1992.

Cardiovascular complications have not been a problem in patients who have experienced severe overdoses of fluoxetine. Seizures have been a problem, as has mild bradycardia. Some studies report atrial dysrhythmia.

4.013. Guze, Barry H., Huan-Kwang Ferng, Martin P. Szuba and Steven Richeimer. "Fluoxetine." in **The Psychiatric Drug Handbook**, by Barry H. Guze, Ferng Huan-Kwang, Martin P. Szuba and Steven Richeimer, 67-70. St. Louis, MO: Mosby Year Book, 1992.

Fluoxetine is administered orally to treat depression, beginning with a dosage of 20 mg/day and increasing this dosage if, after several weeks, there is no clinical improvement. There may be no perceivable antidepressant effect for four weeks or longer. This drug has also been used to treat obsessive-compulsive disorders. Anxiety, insomnia, weight loss, and seizures occur in a relatively small percentage of patients on fluoxetine. MAOIs (monoamine oxidase inhibitors) and fluoxetine should not be combined. Nausea, vomiting, and agitation are major indicators of overdose.

4.014. Judd, Lewis L., Karen Thatcher Briton and David L. Braff. "Fluoxetine." in **Harrison's Principles of Internal Medicine,** Thirteenth Edition, edited by Kurt J. Isselbacher, Eugene Braunwald, Jean D. Wilson, Joseph B. Martin, Anthony S. Fauci and Dennis L. Kasper, 2407. New York, NY: McGraw-Hill, 1994.

The antidepressant efficacy of fluoxetine is comparable to that of imipramine. In addition to being available in tablet form - 20 mg/day is the usual recommended dosage - fluoxetine is available in elixir form, if the dosage required is less than 20 mg/day. Fluoxetine has also been used successfully in controlled studies to treat obsessive-compulsive disorders. Sertraline is available in the U.S., may cause less agitation than fluoxetine, has a much shorter half-life, and does not have an active metabolite.

4.015. Kaplan, Harold I. and Benjamin J. Sadock. "Fluoxetine (Prozac)." in **Pocket Handbook of Clinical Psychiatry,** by Harold I. Kaplan and Benjamin J. Sadock, 257-258. Baltimore, MD: Williams and Wilkins, 1990.

Little or no dry mouth, dizziness, and constipation are some of the side effects typical of tricyclics. These side effects do not apply to fluoxetine. However, fluoxetine does cause weight loss, alertness, insomnia, nervousness, and nausea. This drug may also slightly decrease the pulse rate. Nevertheless, fluoxetine is a first-choice antidepressant drug.

4.016. Loebl, Suzanne, George R. Spratto and Adrienne L. Woods. "Fluoxetine Hydrochloride." in **The Nurse's Drug Handbook,** Seventh Edition, by Suzanne Loebl, George R. Spratto and Adrienne L. Woods, 681-682. N.p., Delmar, 1994.

Fluoxetine, which is not related chemically to other antidepressants, metabolizes to form the metabolite norfluoxetine. The liver further metabolizes norfluoxetine to form inactive metabolites. Fluoxetine and norfluoxetine are, until this time, equally potent. The kidneys excrete the inactive metabolites.

4.017. Long, James W. "Fluoxetine." in **The Essential Guide to Prescription Drugs**, by James W. Long, 484-487. New York, NY: HarperCollins, 1993.

The antidepressant fluoxetine was introduced in 1978. The brand name is Prozac. A prescription is required in the U.S. to obtain this drug, which is not available as a generic. Fluoxetine may be taken without concern about food. However, alcohol should be avoided. This drug may inhibit orgasm in some men and women. There is no habit-forming potential with fluoxetine.

4.018. Mark, Vernon H. and Jeffrey P. Mark. "Antidepressants and Memory Loss." in **Reversing Memory Loss: Proven Methods for Regaining, Strengthening, and Preserving Your Memory**, by Vernon H. Mark and Jeffrey P. Mark, 89-90. Boston, MA: Houghton Mifflin, 1992.

A fifty-seven-year-old female patient whose memory deteriorated while she took Elavil improved when she stopped taking this drug and was given Prozac. Although both Elavil and Prozac can be helpful drugs, no single drug is necessarily of equal benefit to every patient.

4.019. "Prozac." in **1993 Compendium of Pharmaceuticals and Specialties**, Twenty-Eighth Edition, 1002-1003. Ottawa, ON: Canadian Pharmaceutical Association, 1993.

4.020. Schaul, Neil, Gustav Degreef and Gershon C. Ney. "Fluoxetine." in **Adverse Effects of Psychotropic Drugs**, edited by John M. Kane and Jeffrey A. Lieberman, 330-331. New York, NY: Guilford Press, 1992.

When fluoxetine is administered at therapeutic dosages, the incidence of seizures appears to be extremely low. Fluoxetine, rarely associated with seizures, appears to have an overdose incidence similar to or lower than that of tricyclic antidepressants.

4.021. Stoudemire, Alan, Barry S. Fogel, Lawrence R. Gulley and Michael G. Moran. "Fluoxetine." in **Psychiatric Care of the Medical Patient**, edited by Alan Stoudemire and Barry S. Fogel, 163-165. New York, NY: Oxford University Press, 1993.

There has not been any indication of cardiotoxicity in cases of overdose with fluoxetine. This drug is benign even in individuals who have significant cardiovascular illness. Cirrhosis affects the metabolism of fluoxetine, substantially reducing the elimination of this drug. Less-than-daily dosage is necessary for elderly patients. Care should be exercised when administering fluoxetine to epileptics because this drug infrequently provokes seizures.

4.022. Tollefson, Gary D. "Fluoxetine Hydrochloride." in **Current Psychiatric Therapy**, edited by David L. Dunner, 198-199. Philadelphia, PA: W.B. Saunders, 1993.

4.023. Watsky, Eric and Carl Salzman. "Adverse Atypical Antidepressant Drug Interactions - Bupropion, Fluoxetine, and Trazodone." in **Clinical Geriatric Psychopharmacology**, Second Edition, edited by Carl Salzman, 311. Baltimore, MD: Williams and Wilkins, 1992.

This appendix relates in two columns the drug(s) interacting with atypical antidepressant(s) and the clinical effect of the interaction with the atypical antidepressant(s).

4.024. Wood, Philip and C. Mark Castleden. "Table 9.3: Serotonin Agonists." in **Psychiatry in the Elderly**, edited by Robin Jacoby and Catherine Oppenheimer, 352. Oxford: Oxford University Press, 1991.

Fluoxetine, fluvoxamine, and paroxetine are compared in a number of ways, including in terms of absorption, elimination, and plasma binding (per cent).

4.025. Yudofsky, Stuart, Robert E. Hales and Tom Ferguson. "Fluoxetine." in **What You Need to Know about Psychiatric Drugs**, by Stuart Yudofsky, Robert E. Hales and Tom Ferguson, 452-454. New York, NY: Grove Weidenfeld, 1991.

The person taking fluoxetine should inform their physician if they are taking any other drug or vitamin. Three or four weeks may pass before the person on fluoxetine feels the effects of this drug. Double doses should not be taken and fluoxetine should not be discontinued abruptly. This medication should be kept in a tightly-closed container, away from heat, light, and moisture.

REVIEW PAPERS

4.026. Beasley, Charles M., Daniel N. Masica and Janet H. Potvin. "Fluoxetine: A Review of Receptor and Functional

Effects and Their Clinical Implications." **Psychopharmacology** 107 (May 1992): 1-10.

4.027. Ciraulo, Domenic A. and Richard I. Shader. "Fluoxetine Drug-Drug Interactions: I. Antidepressants and Antipsychotics." **Journal of Clinical Psychopharmacology** 10 (February 1990): 48-50.

Many clinicians use fluoxetine not only in the effective treatment of depression, but also in the treatment of obsessive-compulsive disorders. Fluoxetine may interact with other antidepressants. It appears fluoxetine inhibits drug metabolism. The manufacturer of fluoxetine recommends not administering MAOI (monoamine oxidase inhibitor) therapy to patients on fluoxetine, until five weeks after discontinuation of fluoxetine. Author biographical information. 13 references.

4.028. Ciraulo, Domenic A. and Richard I. Shader. "Fluoxetine Drug-Drug Interactions. II. **Journal of Clinical Psychopharmacology** 10 (June 1990): 213-217.

In the U.S. in 1989, $350 million was spent on fluoxetine, thus indicating this drug's acceptance. Buspirone, carbamazepine, fenfluramine, and lithium are some of the drugs with which fluoxetine interacts. The interaction may enhance therapeutic response or may produce toxicity. Author biographical information. 40 references.

4.029. De Vane, C. Lindsay. "Pharmacokinetics of the Selective Serotonin Reuptake Inhibitors." **Journal of Clinical Psychiatry Supplement** 53 (February 1992); 13-20.

Four serotonin reuptake inhibitors - paroxetine, fluvoxamine, fluoxetine, and sertraline - are similar kinetically to older tricyclic antidepressants. These four drugs - well-absorbed orally and widely distributed in body tissues - undergo almost exclusively hepatic metabolism. Fluoxetine has the largest elimination half-life - two to three days. It takes weeks for fluoxetine to achieve steady state. Author biographical information. Abstract. 3 tables. 2 figures. 59 references.

4.030. "Fluoxetine, Suicide and Aggression." **Drug and Therapeutics Bulletin** 30 (January 20, 1992): 5-6.

4.031. Guimaraes, F.S. "Fluoxetine and Fluvoxamine." **British Journal of Hospital Medicine** 45 (March 1991): 146 and 149.

According to most clinical studies, fluoxetine facilitates weight loss. This drug is probably safer in overdose than the tricyclic antidepressants. Its effectiveness is comparable to the effectiveness of imipramine and amitriptyline. In nine out of ten double-blind, short-term, controlled studies of four to six weeks, fluoxetine was superior to placebo in treating major depression. Author biographical information. 1 figure. 4 tables. 6 references.

4.032. Hamilton, Margaret S. and Lewis A. Opler. "Akathisia, Suicidality, and Fluoxetine." **Journal of Clinical Psychiatry** 53 (November 1992): 401-406.

4.033. Power, A.C. and P.J. Cowen. "Fluoxetine and Suicidal Behaviour: Some Clinical and Theoretical Aspects of a Controversy." **British Journal of Psychiatry** 161 (December 1992): 735-741.

Chapter 5

DEPRESSION IN THE ARTS, ENTERTAINMENT, AND POLITICS

BOOKS FOR PROFESSIONALS AND THE GENERAL PUBLIC

5.001. Cronkite, Kathy. **On the Edge of Darkness: Conversations about Conquering Depression.** New York, NY: Doubleday, 1994.

Kathy Cronkite, daughter of CBS anchorman Walter Cronkite, provides accounts of depression experienced by a number of notable individuals. These persons represent entertainment, academic, literary, and political spheres. Joan Rivers, John Kenneth Galbraith, William Styron, and Kitty Dukakis are a few of these notables. Joan Rivers contemplated shooting herself after the suicide of her husband and after she was fired from her television show. Rod Steiger was depressed to the point he was afraid he would use a shotgun to kill his wife then himself. Author Cronkite experienced decades of depression.

5.002. Haynal, Andre. **Depression and Creativity.** New York, NY: International Universities Press, 1985. Originally published as **Le sens du désespoir,** Presses Universitaires de France, 1976.

5.003. Knauth, Percy. **A Season in Hell.** New York, NY: Harper and Row, 1975.

Writer/editor Percy Knauth describes his struggle with deep depression in his autobiography, **A Season in Hell.** Knauth, at age fifty-seven, decided to kill himself by taking an overdose of pills. He did not, at this point, fear death. Suicide seemed to be the logical option. Professional help and a great deal of introspection prevented him from committing suicide.

5.004. Milligan, Spike and Anthony Clare. **Depression and How to Survive It.** London: Ebury, 1993.

About 3 million people in Britain suffer from depression at any one time. Nearly 4,000 people, while severely depressed, commit suicide annually in Britain. The Royal College of

Psychiatrists began in 1992 a Defeat Depression Campaign. Examples of well-known persons who have been afflicted with depression: (1) television personality Ted Moult (shot himself fatally; (2) prize-winning pianist John Ogdon; (3) Oscar-winning actress Brenda Fricker; (4) poet Robert Lowell; (5) former President of the Royal College of General Practitioners Dr. John Horder; (6) Leader of the House of Lords David Waddington; and (7) comic writer and performer Spike Milligan. Milligan has lived with depression for over forty years. He has been occasionally hospitalized and has received electroconvulsive therapy (ECT).

5.005. Moore, Brian. **I Am Mary Dunne.** Toronto, ON: McClelland and Stewart, 1968.

Canadian writer Brian Moore crafted a study of insanity in his book, **I Am Mary Dunne.** Mary Dunne is a fictitious character based on a real-life woman Moore was in love with and who experienced PMS (premenstrual syndrome). Mary Dunne is on the verge of madness. Moore views depression associated with PMS as a societally acceptable type of madness.

5.006. Sanders, Lawrence. **The Third Deadly Sin.** New York, NY: Berkeley Books, 1982.

Zoe Kohler is a psychotic female who suffers from premenstrual syndrome (PMS) and who, in this best-selling murder mystery, kills six men in their hotel rooms.

5.007. Styron, William. **Darkness Visible: A Memoir of Madness.** New York, NY: Random House, 1990.

Novelist William Styron, recipient of the Pulitzer prize and the American Book Award, began, during the summer of 1985, to experience persistent insomnia and troubling malaise. These were the first indicators of a deep depression. Styron spoke about his depression in May 1989 in Baltimore, Maryland at a symposium on affective disorders. He expanded his symposium lecture into an essay which was published in the December 1989 issue of **Vanity Fair.**

5.008. Thorne, Julia and Larry Rothstein. **You Are Not Alone: Words of Experience and Hope for the Journey through Depression.** New York, NY: HarperCollins, 1993.

Julia Thorne, a poet and writer residing in Brookline, Massachusetts, survived eight years of depression to establish The Depression Initiative, a nonprofit educational organization.

CHAPTERS AND SECTIONS IN BOOKS FOR PROFESSIONALS AND THE GENERAL PUBLIC

5.009. Butler, Pamela. "Depression: The Consequences of Nonrecognition." in **Self-Assertion for Women,** New Edition, by Pamela Butler, 32-34. San Francisco, CA: Harper and Row, 1981.

Zelda Fitzgerald, wife of F. Scott Fitzgerald, needed and wanted recognition for her writing talents. Her needs were not in accord with the then feminine role. Her husband received credit in his book for her ideas and portions of her letters. Most of Zelda's married life was characterized by nonrecognition, nonreinforcement, depression.

5.010. Byck, Robert. "Depression." Chapter in **Treating Mental Illness,** by Robert Byck, 53-64. New York, NY: Chelsea House Publishers, 1986.

Albrecht Dürer, the sixteenth-century German painter and engraver, depicted depression in his work entitled "Melancholia." The corporate world, according to an interpretation of the House of Stairs, a 1951 lithograph by Mauritis Cornelis Escher, causes acute anxiety and depression. Poet Anne Sexton, author of **Live or Die,** committed suicide in 1974. The Pulitzer prize-winning poet had struggled with a series of depressions. Roland Kuhn, a Swiss psychiatrist, learned, during research in 1957, that imipramine had a positive effect on depressed patients, after they were treated for a few weeks with this drug. 8 figures.

5.011. Carroll, John. "Depressive Guilt." Chapter in **Guilt: The Grey Eminence Behind Character, History and Culture,** by John Carroll, 68-94. London: Routledge and Kegan Paul, 1985.

5.012. Dabrowski, Kazimierz. "Creative Depression." in **The Dynamics of Concepts,** by Kazimierz Dabrowski, 156-158. London: Gryf Publications, 1973.

There are in the majority of depressive states both pathological and positive elements. Emotions such as shame and guilt are factors in a person's progression to higher mental development. Depression is frequently encountered when former ways of experiencing the world become inadequate. The search by prominent individuals - Soren Kierkegaard and Vincent van Gogh are two examples - for creative expression was accompanied by depression.

5.013. Geller, Anne and M.J. Territo. "Depression." in **Restore Your Life: A Living Plan for Sober People,** by Anne Geller and M.J. Territo, 95-97. New York, NY: Bantam Books, 1991.

Actress Holly Hunter plays in the movie **Broadcast News** a conscientious and ambitious news producer by the name of Jane Craig. About the only time Jane is not depressed is when she is busy. Physical or mental activity can help some depressed people in real-life situations.

5.014. Gleitman, Henry. "Depression." in **Psychology,** by Henry Gleitman, 682-683. New York, NY: W.W. Norton and Company, 1981.

It is in Act I, Scene ii of **Hamlet** that Prince Hamlet talks about his preoccupation with death and suicide.

5.015. Hofling, Charles K. "The Treatment of Depression: A Selective Historical Review." Chapter in **Depression: Clinical, Biological and Psychological Perspectives,** edited by Gene Usdin, 52-72. New York, NY: Brunner/Mazel, 1977.

There is in the **Old Testament** an account of what today would likely be designated as a psychotic depression. The account refers to King Saul's madness and is given in I Samuel, chapters 15-31. The Greek physician Hippocrates (460?-?377 B.C.); Greek philosopher Aristotle (384-322 B.C.); and Greek physician and writer Galen (130-200) also contributed to historical thought about depression. **The Anatomy of Melancholy** by Robert Burton (1577-1640) was published in 1621. This work contains, in part, selected ideas of Christopher Marlowe (1564-1593), William Shakespeare (1564-1616), and John Donne (1572-1631). 19 references. General Bibliography (14 publications).

5.016. Meyers, J. "Hemingway." in **Life-Span Development,** Fourth Edition, by John W. Santrock, 602. Dubuque, IA: Wm. C. Brown, 1992.

Ernest Hemingway, whose father committed suicide, seemed to be obsessed with the idea of self-destruction. He sometimes had suicidal thoughts when he had a marital crisis. Hemingway, in his sixties and suffering because of physical and mental illnesses, killed himself with a shotgun. He had been severely depressed and had dreaded becoming an invalid. 2 photographs.

5.017. Rosenblatt, Seymour and Reynolds Dodson. "Depression - Of Cheddar Cheese and Darwin." Chapter in **Beyond Valium: The**

Brave New World of Psychochemistry, by Seymour Rosenblatt and Reynolds Dodson, 80-101. New York, NY: G.P. Putnam's Sons, 1981.

Chemicals were used to produce shock treatments prior to the use of electricity. Insulin and camphor were used to create convulsions. Movies like **The Snake Pit** and **One Flew over the Cuckoo's Nest** have unjustly given electroconvulsive treatment (ECT) a negative image. The respective cure rates for depression are: drugs, 70% to 80%; placebos, 20% to 30%; and ECT, 90% plus.

5.018. Rubin, Zick and Elton B. McNeil. "Depression." in **The Psychology of Being Human,** Third Edition, by Zick Rubin and Elton B. McNeil, 377-380. New York, NY: Harper and Row, 1983.

Winston Churchill, Abraham Lincoln, and Vincent van Gogh are examples of famous individuals who suffered from depression. 1 photograph.

5.019. Snyder, Solomon H. "Depression: A Sad Disease." Chapter in **The Troubled Mind: A Guide to Release from Distress,** by Solomon H. Snyder, 50-70. New York, NY: McGraw-Hill, 1976.

Depression is not a condition of modern times because it was described by people such as Hippocrates and Plutarch. Tolstoy wrote about his own depression. German psychiatrist Emil Kraepelin, in the late 1800s, conceived the idea of manic-depressive illness. John Custance, a British writer, gave an autobiographical account of manic-depressive psychosis. An environmental event will precipitate exogenous (neurotic) depression, while a predisposition in a person will precipitate endogenous (psychotic) depression.

5.020. Solomon, Robert C. "Depression." in **The Passions,** by Robert C. Solomon, 296-300. Garden City, NY: Anchor Press/ Doubleday, 1976.

5.021. Storr, Anthony. "Creativity and the Manic-Depressive Temperament." Chapter in **The Dynamics of Creation,** by Anthony Storr, 75-91. New York, NY: Atheneum, 1972.

Artist Michelangelo, composer Robert Schumann, and novelist Balzac are examples of famous manic-depressives. 14 references.

5.022. Warshaw, Leon J. "Depression." in **Managing Stress,** by Leon J. Warshaw, 146. Reading, MA: Addison-Wesley, 1979.

Willy Loman in Arthur Miller's play, **Death of a Salesman**, typifys the depressed person, who is prematurely old and, among other things, has dreams that cannot become realities.

5.023. Watson, David L. "Electro-Convulsive Therapy." in **Psychology**, by David L. Watson, 564. Pacific Grove, CA: Brooks/Cole, 1992.

Hemingway in **A Farewell to Arms** wrote about doctors doing things to a person's body until the body was no longer a person's original body. During a one-month period, during which he was hospitalized, Hemingway was administered eleven electroconvulsive (ECT) treatments. This treatment for depression, although effective, can bring about permanent memory loss, something which greatly disturbed Hemingway.

5.024. Watson, David L. "Mood Disorders." in **Psychology**, by David L. Watson, 509-514. Pacific Grove, CA: Brooks/Cole, 1992.

Several other family members in Ernest Hemingway's family experienced severe depression: his father, brother, and sister. Hemingway had often talked about suicide, having tried several times to kill himself before succeeding. Although he had accomplished much, and was becoming an old man, his life was not ruined. Hemingway had written about suicide in his short story "Indian Camp."

Appendix A

UNITED STATES—DEPRESSION AND RELATED ORGANIZATIONS—ADDRESSES AND PUBLICATIONS

1. American Psychiatric Association
   1400 K Street N.W.
   WASHINGTON, DC
   20005

   BOOKLETS

   Let's Talk Facts about Depression (20 pages)

2. Center for Cognitive Therapy
   University of Pennsylvania
   Room 754
   The Science Center
   3600 Market Street
   PHILADELPHIA, Pennsylvania
   19104-2648

3. Dave Garroway Laboratory for the Study of Depression
   111 North 49th Street
   Pennsylvania Hospital
   PHILADELPHIA, Pennsylvania
   19139

4. Depression after Delivery
   P.O. Box 1282
   MORRISVILLE, Pennsylvania
   19067

   MINI-JOURNALS

   Postpartum Equilibria

   NEWSLETTERS

   Heart and Strings
   Genesis

   BROCHURES

   Feelings after Birth: Postpartum Adjustment

5. Depression and Related Affective Disorders Association, Inc.
Johns Hopkins Hospital, Meyer 4-181
1601 North Wolfe Street
BALTIMORE, Maryland
21205

NEWSLETTERS

Smooth Sailing

6. The Foundation for Depression and Manic Depression, Inc.
7 East 67th Street
NEW YORK, New York
10021

NEWSLETTERS

The Foundation Newsletter

BOOKLETS

The Depressive Disorders (20 pages)

FACT SHEETS

Bipolar Disorder (Manic-Depressive Illness) (2 pages)

Major Depression (3 pages)

7. Los Angeles Center for Cognitive Therapy
630 South Wilton Place
LOS ANGELES, California
90005

NEWSLETTERS

Emery News

8. National Alliance for Research on Schizophrenia and Depression
60 Cutter Mill Road, Suite 200
GREAT NECK, New York
11021

NEWSLETTERS

NARSAD Research Newsletter

BOOKLETS

NARSAD Research: Grantee Listing by University or Research Center (12 pages)

The Search for Cures (8 pages)

9. National Depressive and Manic-Depressive Association
730 North Franklin, Suite 501
CHICAGO, Illinois
60610

BOOKLETS

Depressive Illness: The Medical Facts The Human Challenge (10 pages)

If You Suspect Someone You Care about Is Considering Suicide (8 pages)

Just a Mood...Or Real Depression? (8 pages)

Suicide and Depressive Illness (8 pages)

When Treatments Fail: Depression and Manic-Depression (8 pages)

BROCHURES

National Depressive and Manic-Depressive Association

FACT SHEETS

National DMDA Fact Sheet (1 page)

Depressive and Manic-Depressive Illness (2 pages)

10. National Foundation for Depressive Illness, Inc.
P.O. Box 2257
NEW YORK, New York
10116

NEWSLETTERS

NAFDI News

BOOKLETS

Now We Can Successfully Treat the Illness Called Depression (8 pages)

11. National Institute of Mental Health
5600 Fishers Lane
ROCKVILLE, Maryland
20857

BOOKLETS

Depression: What You Need to Know. Publication No. ADM 91-1543 (10 pages)

Depressive Illnesses: Treatments Bring New Hope. Publication No. NIH 93-3612 (38 pages)

Diagnosis and Treatment of Depression in Late Life. Publication No. OM 00-4084 (27 pages)

Electro-Convulsive Therapy. Publication No. OM 00-4018 (8 pages)

Helpful Facts about Depressive Disorders. Publication No. ADM 92-1536 (8 pages)

Helping the Depressed Person Get Treatment. Publication No. ADM 90-1675 (23 pages)

If You're over 65 and Feeling Depressed...Treatment Brings New Hope. Publication No. ADM 90-1653 (12 pages)

Information about D/ART and Depression. Publication No. ADM 91-1873 (16 pages)

Lithium. Publication No. NIH 93-3476 (18 pages)

Mood Disorders: Pharmacologic Prevention of Recurrences. Publication No. OM 00-4015 (8 pages)

Plain Talk about Depression. NIH 93-3561 (4 pages)

FOLD-OUTS

Bipolar Disorder: Manic-Depressive Illness. Publication No. ADM 90-1609 (6-panel folder)

Depression: Effective Treatments Are Available. Publication No. ADM 92-1652

Let's Talk about Depression. Publication No. ADM 91-1695 (6-panel folder)

Managing Depression in the Workplace. Publication No. ADM 91-1793 (pocket folder)

What to Do When an Employee Is Depressed: A Guide for Supervisors. Publication No. ADM 91-1792 (6-panel folder)

FOLD-OUT/POSTER

What to Do When a Friend Is Depressed: Guide for Students. Publication No. ADM 92-1628 (6-panel folder)

POSTER

Not Everyone with Depression Is This Visible. Publication No. ADM 91-1871 (16½ X 22). ADM 91-1872 (8½ X 11)

12. National Mental Health Association
1021 Prince Street
ALEXANDRIA, Virginia
22314-2971

BOOKLETS

Answers to Your Questions about Clinical Depression (16 pages)

FACT SHEETS

Causes of Depression (2 pages)

Helping Children Cope with Depression in the Family (2 pages)

Helping Depressed Adults (2 pages)

Helping Depressed Children and Adolescents (2 pages)

Holiday Depression and Stress (1 page)

Recognizing Adolescent Depression (1 page)

Recognizing Depression (2 pages)

Seasonal Affective Disorder (1 page)

What Is Depression? (2 pages)

Who Gets Depression? (2 pages)

13. University of Iowa
Affective Disorders Research Unit
Department of Psychiatry
500 Newton Road
IOWA CITY, Iowa
52242

14. University of Pennsylvania
Depression Research Unit
University City Science Center
3600 Market Street, 8th Floor
PHILADELPHIA, Pennsylvania
19104-2649

Appendix B

CANADA—DEPRESSION AND RELATED ORGANIZATIONS—ADDRESSES AND PUBLICATIONS

1. Canadian Group Psychotherapy Foundation
   72 Barrie Street
   KINGSTON, Ontario
   K7L 3J7

2. Canadian Mental Health Association
   2160 Yonge Street, 3rd Floor
   TORONTO, Ontario
   M4S 2Z3

   BROCHURES

   Depression and Manic-Depression

3. Depressed Anonymous, Inc.
   1111 Stellar Drive, Suite 4B
   Stellar Walker Centre
   NEWMARKET, Ontario
   L3Y 7B8

4. Depressive and Manic-Depressive Association of Ontario
   214 Merton Street, Suite 101
   TORONTO, Ontario
   M4S 1A6

   NEWSLETTERS

   The Link

5. Depressive and Manic-Depressive Self-Help Group of Durham Region
   275 Ormond Drive, Suite 46
   OSHAWA, Ontario
   L1K 1S1

6. Manic-Depressive Association for the Region of Peel
   150 Clark Boulevard, Suite 87
   BRAMPTON, Ontario
   L6T 4Y8

NEWSLETTERS

MDARP Newsletter

7. Manic-Depressive Association of Metropolitan Toronto
40 Orchard View Boulevard, Suite 252
TORONTO, Ontario
M4R 1B9

NEWSLETTERS

MDAMT Newsletter

8. Manic-Depressive Association (Simcoe)
c/o Simcoe County Public Health
370 Dunlop Street West, Suite 1201
BARRIE, Ontario
L4N 5R7

9. Vancouver Island Depressive and Manic-Depressive Association
P.O. Box 5787
Station B
VICTORIA, B.C.
V8R 6S8

Appendix C

GREAT BRITAIN—DEPRESSION AND RELATED ORGANIZATIONS—ADDRESSES AND PUBLICATIONS

1. The Association for Postnatal Illness
   25 Jerdan Place
   Fulham, London
   SW6 1BE
   England

   BOOKLETS

   A Guide to Prophylactic Progesterone for Postnatal Depression (10 pages)

   Postnatal Depression (12 pages)

   Postnatal Depression Doctors' Notes for Guidance (12 pages)

   Postnatal Depression Health Visitors' Notes for Guidance (12 pages)

   LEAFLETS

   The Baby Blues and Postnatal Depression (4 pages)

   Puerperal Psychosis (4 pages)

2. British Association for Counselling
   37a Sheep Street
   Rugby, Warwickshire
   CV21 3BX
   England

3. The Manic-Depression Fellowship
   13 Rosslyn Road
   Twickenham, Middlesex
   TW1 2AR
   England

4. MIND
22 Harley Street
London
W1N 2ED
England

5. RELATE (Marriage Guidance Council)
Herbert Gray College
Little Church Street
Rugby
CV21 3AP
England

6. The Samaritans
17 Uxbridge Road
Slough, Berks
SL1 1SN
England

Appendix D

IRELAND—DEPRESSION AND RELATED ORGANIZATIONS—ADDRESSES AND PUBLICATIONS

1. AWARE
   Information Centre
   147 Phibsborough Road
   Dublin 7
   Ireland

   MAGAZINES

   Awareness

   BROCHURES

   Better Understanding through Increased Awareness

   Depression in the Workplace

   1994 Dublin Lectures

   1994 Nationwide Support Group Meetings

2. GROW
   11 Liberty Street, Cork and 50 Middle Abbey Street
   Dublin 1
   Ireland

3. The Mental Health Association of Ireland
   Mensana House
   6 Adelaide Street
   Dun Laoghaire
   Co. Dublin
   Ireland

Appendix E

VIDEOCASSETTE DISTRIBUTORS/PRODUCERS—ADDRESSES

1. AEF/Capital Communications
   3807 Dickerson Road
   NASHVILLE, Tennessee
   37207

2. American Journal of Nursing Company
   Educational Services Division
   555 West 57th Street
   NEW YORK, New York
   10019-2961

3. American Medical Association
   Department of Marketing Communications
   515 North State Street
   CHICAGO, Illinois
   60610

4. Barr Films
   12801 Schabarum
   IRWINDALE, California
   91706

5. Cinema Guild
   1697 Broadway, Suite 802
   NEW YORK, New York
   10019

6. CRM/McGraw-Hill Films
   674 Via de la Valle
   P.O. Box 641
   DEL MAR, California
   92014

7. Filmakers Library, Inc.
   124 East 40th Street
   NEW YORK, New York
   10016

8. Films for the Humanities
   P.O. Box 2053
   PRINCETON, New Jersey
   08543

9. Milner-Fenwick, Inc.
   2125 Greenspring Drive
   TIMONIUM, Maryland
   21093-9989

10. MPI Home Video
    15825 Rob Roy Drive
    OAK FOREST, Illinois
    60452

11. Professional Research, Inc.
    1560 Sherman, Suite 100
    EVANSTON, Illinois
    60201

12. United Learning, Inc.
    6633 West Howard Street
    NILES, Illinois
    60648

13. University of Texas
    M.D. Anderson Cancer Center
    1515 Holcombe
    HOUSTON, Texas
    77030

Appendix F

TELEVISION PROGRAMS

1. "Baby Blues." **The Maury Povich Show.** July 23, 1992.
2. "Brain Storms - Causes of Depression, Part 2." **Newsday** (CNN), May 19, 1993.
3. "Brain Storms - Efforts to Treat Mental Illness, Part 3." **Newsday** (CNN), May 20, 1993
4. "Chronic Fatigue Syndrome May Be Linked to Depression." **Early Prime** (CNN), September 15, 1992.
5. "Depression Has Different Causes and Cures." **Morning News** (CNN), September 22, 1992.
6. "Kitty Dukakis - Free from Addiction." **Larry King Live** (CNN), June 6, 1991.
7. "Major Problem - Depression and Manic-Depressive Illness." **Morning News** (CNN), May 17, 1993.
8. "Many Well-Known Actors Deal with Manic-Depression." **Early Prime** (CNN), November 30, 1993.
9. "Octogenarian May Be Forced to Undergo Shock Treatment." **Morning Edition** (NPR), January 21, 1994.
10. "Out of the Black Hole." **20/20** (ABC), August 14, 1992.
11. "Patty Duke - A Healthy New Start." **Larry King Live** (CNN), June 10, 1992.
12. "The Shocking Truth - Electroshock Therapy." **Geraldo.** November 30, 1990.
13. "'A State of Mind' - County Official Is Manic-Depressive." **DAY ONE** (ABC), February 14, 1994.
14. "'Winter Blues' Treatment Tied to Body's Internal Clock." **Newsnight** (CNN), August 11, 1993.

For additional information about the preceding contact:

Journal Graphics, Inc.
1535 Grant Street
DENVER, Colorado
80203

15. "Analysis: A Look at Various Treatments for Depression." **CBS This Morning** (CBS), August 7, 1992.

16. "Interview: Actress Patty Duke on Her Battle with Manic-Depression." **NBC Today** (NBC), June 9, 1992.

17. "Interview: Change in Seasons Threatens My Marriage; Three Patients Say They Suffer from Seasonal Affective Disorder." **Jane Whitney Show** (BNO), July 27, 1994.

18. "Interview: Dr. Roger Greenberg, Dr. Jack Gorman on Prozac." **NBC Sunday Today** (NBC), May 13, 1990.

19. "Interview: Ellen McGrath Discusses Depression." **CBS This Morning** (CBS), March 23, 1992.

20. "Interview: Eric Hollander, Columbia University; Holiday Depression." **NBC Saturday Today** (NBC), December 19, 1992.

21. "Interview: Guests Discuss How Prozac Affected Their Sex Lives." **Real Personal** (CNBC), April 5, 1994.

22. "Profile: Economic Recession Can Lead to Mental Depression." **CBS This Morning** (CBS), December 31, 1990.

23. "Profile: Extended Postpartum Depression Requires Professional Support." **CBS This Morning** (CBS), August 16, 1994.

24. "Profile: Ups and Downs; Prozac Becoming Drug of Choice for Variety of Illnesses and Experts Fear It Will Be Abused." **Eye to Eye with Connie Chung** (CBS), December 23, 1993.

For additional information about the above contact:

Burrelle's Transcripts
P.O. Box 7
LIVINGSTON, New Jersey
07039-0007

Appendix G

COMPUTERS IN DEPRESSION RESEARCH

1. DeWolfe, Alan S., Jacquelyn K. Larson and Joseph J. Ryan. "Diagnostic Accuracy of the Millon Test Computer Reports for Bipolar Affective Disorder." **Journal of Psychopathology and Behavioral Assessment** 7 (September 1985): 185-189.

2. Falk, Marshall A. "The Computer Analyzes Two Psychotherapeutic Agents in Anxiety/Depressed States." **Current Therapeutic Research** 15 (July 1973): 488-499.

3. Glaze, R. and J.L. Cox. "Validation of a Computerised Version of the 10-Item (Self-Rating) Edinburgh Postnatal Depression Scale." **Journal of Affective Disorders** 22 (May-June 1991): 73-77.

4. Gonzalez, Gerardo M. "Computerized Speech Recognition in Psychological Assessment: A Macintosh Prototype for Screening Depressive Symptoms." **Behavior Research Methods, Instruments and Computers** 25 (May 1993): 301-303.

5. Kobak, Kenneth A., William M. Reynolds, Rachelli Rosenfeld and John H. Greist. "Development and Validation of a Computer-Administered Version of the Hamilton Depression Rating Scale." **Psychological Assessment** 2 (March 1990): 56-63.

6. MacLean, Alistair W., John B. Knowles and Charles Vetere. "REM Sleep and Depression: Further Use of Computer Simulation to Test the Phase-Advance Hypothesis." **Psychiatry Research** 19 (September 1986): 25-36.

7. Margo, A., C. Johnson, R. Ancill and T. Carr. "Assessment of Depression by Microcomputer." **Acta Psychiatrica Scandinavica** 67 (June 1983): 434-435.

8. Maurer, Kurt, Hugo Biehl, C. Kuhner and W. Loffler. "On the Way to Expert Systems: Comparing DSM-III Computer Diagnoses with CATEGO (ICD) Diagnoses in Depressive and Schizophrenic Patients." **European Archives of Psychiatry and Neurological Sciences** 239 (September 1989): 127-132.

9. McLean, P.C., R.J. Ancill and T.K. Szulecka. "Mianserin in the Treatment of Depressive Symptoms in Alcoholics: A Double-Blind Placebo Controlled Study Using a Computer Delivered Self-Rating Scale." **Psychiatria Polska** 20 (November-December 1986): 417-427.

10. Sarteschi, P., G.B. Cassano, P. Castrogiovanni and L. Conti. "The Use of Rating Scales for Computer Analysis of the Affective Symptoms in Old Age." **Comprehensive Psychiatry** 14 (July 1973): 371-379.

11. Selmi, Paulette, Marjorie H. Klein, John H. Greist, Steven P. Sorrell and Harold P. Erdman. "Computer-Administered Cognitive-Behavioral Therapy for Depression." **American Journal of Psychiatry** 147 (January 1990): 51-56.

Appendix H

PSYCHOLOGICAL ABSTRACTS

DATABASE NAME	PSYCINFO
CD-ROM EQUIVALENT	PSYCLIT
PRINT EQUIVALENT	**Psychological Abstracts**
DATA PROVIDER	American Psychological Association
PROVIDER ADDRESS	American Psychological Association 750 1st Street N.E. WASHINGTON, DC 20002-4242
SOFTWARE PRODUCER	SilverPlatter Information, Inc.
PRODUCER ADDRESS	SilverPlatter Information, Inc. 100 River Ridge Drive NORWOOD, Massachusetts 02602-5026
MAIN ONLINE VENDORS	DIALOG, BRS
VENDOR ADDRESSES	DIALOG Information Services, Inc. 3460 Hillview Avenue PALO ALTO, California 94304 BRS InfoPro Technologies 8000 Westpark Drive McLEAN, Virginia 22102
NOTES	Contact vendors and software producers regarding user training. The following may vary for online and CD: search commands, time span searchable, connect time costs, and print costs.

Appendix I

INDEX MEDICUS

DATABASE NAME	MEDLINE
CD-ROM EQUIVALENT	MEDLINE STANDARD
PRINT EQUIVALENT	**Index Medicus** **Index to Dental Literature** **International Nursing Index**
DATA PROVIDER	U.S. National Library of Medicine
PROVIDER ADDRESS	U.S. National Library of Medicine 8600 Rockville Pike BETHESDA, Maryland 20894
SOFTWARE PRODUCER	SilverPlatter Information, Inc.
PRODUCER ADDRESS	SilverPlatter Information, Inc. 100 River Ridge Drive NORWOOD, Massachusetts 02602-5026
MAIN ONLINE VENDORS	DIALOG, BRS
VENDOR ADDRESSES	DIALOG Information Services, Inc. 3460 Hillview Avenue PALO ALTO, California 94304 BRS InfoPro Technologies 8000 Westpark Drive McLEAN, Virginia 22102
NOTES	Contact vendors and software producers regarding user training. The following may vary for online and CD: search commands, time span searchable, connect time costs, and print costs.

Appendix J

SCIENCE CITATION INDEX

DATABASE NAME	SCISEARCH
CD-ROM EQUIVALENT	SCIENCE CITATION INDEX COMPACT DISC EDITION WITH ABSTRACTS
PRINT EQUIVALENT	**Science Citation Index** **Current Contents**
DATA PROVIDER	Institute for Scientific Information
PROVIDER ADDRESS	Institute for Scientific Information 3501 Market Street PHILADELPHIA, Pennsylvania 19104
SOFTWARE PRODUCER	Institute for Scientific Information
PRODUCER ADDRESS	Institute for Scientific Information 3501 Market Street PHILADELPHIA, Pennsylvania 19104
MAIN ONLINE VENDORS	DIALOG, CAN/OLE
VENDOR ADDRESSES	DIALOG Information Services, Inc. 3460 Hillview Avenue PALO ALTO, California 94304 CAN/OLE Canada Institute for Scientific and Technical Information National Research Council Canada OTTAWA, Ontario K1A 0S2
NOTES	Contact vendors and software producers regarding user training. The following may vary for online and CD: search commands, time span searchable, connect time costs, and print costs.

Appendix K

SOCIAL SCIENCES CITATION INDEX

DATABASE NAME	SOCIAL SCISEARCH
CD-ROM EQUIVALENT	SOCIAL SCIENCES CITATION INDEX COMPACT INDEX COMPACT DISC EDITION WITH ABSTRACTS
PRINT EQUIVALENT	**Social Sciences Citation Index**
DATA PROVIDER	Institute for Scientific Information
PROVIDER ADDRESS	Institute for Scientific Information 3501 Market Street PHILADELPHIA, Pennsylvania 19104
SOFTWARE PRODUCER	Institute for Scientific Information
PRODUCER ADDRESS	Institute for Scientific Information 3501 Market Street PHILADELPHIA, Pennsylvania 19104
MAIN ONLINE VENDORS	DIALOG, BRS
VENDOR ADDRESSES	DIALOG Information Services, Inc. 3460 Hillview Avenue PALO ALTO, California 94304 BRS InfoPro Technologies 8000 Westpark Drive McLEAN, Virginia 22102
NOTES	Contact vendors and software producers regarding user training. The following may vary for online and CD: search commands, time span searchable, connect time costs, and print costs.

Appendix L

BIOLOGICAL ABSTRACTS

DATABASE NAME	BIOSIS PREVIEWS
CD-ROM EQUIVALENT	BIOLOGICAL ABSTRACTS ON COMPACT DISC
PRINT EQUIVALENT	**Biological Abstracts**
DATA PROVIDER	BIOSIS
PROVIDER ADDRESS	BIOSIS 2100 Arch Street PHILADELPHIA, Pennsylvania 19103-1399
SOFTWARE PRODUCER	SilverPlatter Information, Inc.
PRODUCER ADDRESS	SilverPlatter Information, Inc. 100 River Ridge Drive NORWOOD, Massachusetts 02602-5026
MAIN ONLINE VENDORS	DIALOG, BRS, CAN/OLE
VENDOR ADDRESSES	DIALOG Information Services, Inc. 3460 Hillview Avenue PALO ALTO, California 94304 BRS InfoPro Technologies 8000 Westpark Drive McLEAN, Virginia 22102 CAN/OLE Canada Institute for Scientific and Technical Information National Research Council Canada OTTAWA, Ontario K1A OS2

NOTES

Contact vendors and software producers regarding user training. The following may vary for online and CD: search commands, time span searchable, connect time costs, and print costs.

Appendix M

DISSERTATION ABSTRACTS

DATABASE NAME	DISSERTATION ABSTRACTS ONLINE
CD-ROM EQUIVALENT	DISSERTATION ABSTRACTS ONDISC
PRINT EQUIVALENT	**Dissertation Abstracts**
DATA PROVIDER	University Microfilms International
PROVIDER ADDRESS	University Microfilms International 300 North Zeeb Road ANN ARBOR, Michigan 48106
SOFTWARE PRODUCER	University Microfilms International
PRODUCER ADDRESS	University Microfilms International 300 North Zeeb Road ANN ARBOR, Michigan 48106
MAIN ONLINE VENDORS	DIALOG, BRS
VENDOR ADDRESSES	DIALOG Information Services, Inc. 3460 Hillview Avenue PALO ALTO, California 94304 BRS InfoPro Technologies 8000 Westpark Drive McLEAN, Virginia 22102
NOTES	Contact vendors and software producers regarding user training. The following may vary for online and CD: search commands, time span searchable, connect time costs, and print costs.

Appendix N

PROZAC—POPULAR ARTICLES

1. Angier, N. "Moody News: Can a Pill Called Prozac End Depression?" **Mademoiselle** 96 (April 1990): 229+.

2. Bowe, C.D. "Women and Depression: Are We Being Overdosed?" **Redbook** 178 (March 1992): 42+.

3. Brink, S. "Singing the Prozac Blues." **U.S. News and World Report** 115 (November 8, 1993): 76-79.

4. Brown, S.A. "Miracle Worker." **People Weekly** 40 (November 15, 1993): 153-155.

5. Clendinen, D. "Prozac 101." **Lear's** 6 (October 1993): 70-73+.

6. "Committee Advises FDA on Antidepressants." **FDA Consumer** 25 (December 1991): 5.

7. Cowley, G. "The Culture of Prozac." **Newsweek** 123 (February 7, 1994): 41-42.

8. Cowley, G. "A Prozac Backlash." **Newsweek** 117 (April 1, 1991): 64-67.

9. Gates, D. "The Case of Dr. Strangedrug." **Newsweek** 121 (June 14, 1993): 71.

10. "Halcion and Prozac." **Consumer Reports** 58 (January 1993): 22.

11. Kramer, P.D. "The Transformation of Personality." **Psychology Today** 26 (July-August 1993): 42-47+.

12. Nichols, Mark. "Questioning Prozac." **Maclean's** 107 (May 23, 1994): 36-39.

13. "The Promise of Prozac." **Newsweek** 115 (March 26, 1990): 38-44.

14. Reiss, S. "A Prescription for a Negative Campaign." **Newsweek** 115 (April 30, 1990): 22.

15. Schumer, F. "Bye-Bye, Blues: A New Wonder Drug for Depression." **New York** 22 (December 18, 1989): 46-50+.

16. Schwartz, J. and B. Cohn. "'The Drug Did It:' A Tough Sell in Court." **Newsweek** 117 (April 1, 1991): 66.

17. Styron, W. "Prozac Days, Halcion Nights." **The Nation** 256 (January 4-11, 1993): 1+.

18. Thompson, T. "Seeking the Wizards of Prozac." **The Saturday Evening Post** 266 (March-April 1994): 50-53+.

19. Toufexis, A. "The Personality Pill." **Time** 142 (October 11, 1993): 61-62.

20. Toufexis, A. "Warnings about a Miracle Drug." **Time** 136 (July 30, 1990): 54.

Appendix O

BIOGRAPHIES/AUTOBIOGRAPHIES OF PROMINENT INDIVIDUALS WITH DEPRESSION

1. Cavett, Dick and Christopher Porterfield. **Eye on Cavett.** New York, NY: Arbor House, 1983.
2. Dukakis, Kitty and Jane Scovell. **Now You Know.** New York, NY: Simon and Schuster, 1990.
3. Duke, Patty and Gloria Hochman. **A Brilliant Madness: Living with Manic-Depressive Illness.** New York, NY: Bantam Books, 1992.
4. Gilbert, Martin. **Churchill: A Life.** London: Heinemann, 1991.
5. Gordon, Lyndall. **Virginia Woolf: A Writer's Life.** Oxford: Oxford University Press, 1984.
6. Hayman, Ronald. **The Death and Life of Sylvia Plath.** New York, NY: Carol Publishing Group, 1991.
7. Lewis, Roger. **The Life and Death of Peter Sellers.** London: Century, 1994.
8. Mellow, James R. **Hemingway: A Life Without Consequences.** Boston, MA: Houghton Mifflin, 1992.
9. Richards, David. **Played Out: The Jean Seberg Story.** New York, NY: Random House, 1981.
10. Sexton, Linda Gray and Lois Ames. Editors. **Anne Sexton: A Self-Portrait in Letters.** Boston, MA: Houghton Mifflin, 1977.

Appendix P

DEPRESSION TIME-LINE

1904	Emil Kraepelin classifies and describes the manic-depressive syndrome.
1912	Classic paper by Karl Abraham on the psychoanalytic investigation and treatment of manic-depressive illness and related conditions.
1917	Classic paper by Sigmund Freud on mourning and melancholia.
1931	Publication by Clifford W. Beers of his autobiography, **A Mind That Found Itself.**
1936	Amphetamines are among the first classes of drugs used to treat depression.
1938	Ugo Cerletti and Lucio Bini develop the first effective electroshock therapy.
1949	John Cade discovers lithium.
1958	Imipramine, the first tricyclic antidepresant, is introduced.
1961	Monoamine oxidase inhibitors (MAOIs) are introduced.
	The Beck Depression Inventory (BDI) is introduced.
	Ernest Hemingway commits suicide.
1964	Martin Seligman begins research on learned helplessness.
1969	Rowell Laboratories begin to commercially market lithium.
1971	Wyatt v. Stickney landmark case upholds the right of a mentally ill person to treatment, including the right to refuse ECT (electroconvulsive treatment).

1972 Senator Thomas P. Eagleton withdraws as Democratic candidate for U.S. Vice-President, after it is revealed he had been hospitalized for depression and received shock therapy.

1974 Poet Anne Sexton commits suicide.

1987 Prozac, a selective serotonin reuptake inhibitor (SSRI), is introduced.

1989 Novelist William Styron discusses his depression at an affective disorders conference in Baltimore, Maryland.

1991 Sertraline is introduced.

1992 The Royal College of Psychiatrists in Britain begins the "Defeat Depression Campaign."

1993 Paxil, another SSRI, is introduced.

AUTHOR INDEX

Includes Authors, Coauthors, Editors, and Translators.

Numbers Below Are Page Numbers, Not Entry Numbers.

SUBJECT INDEX

About the Compiler

JOHN J. MILETICH is former Reference Librarian, University of Alberta. He has published book-length bibliographies in psychology, medical studies, sociology, and gerontology.